Shocking Celebrity Murders

True Crime Cases of Famous People Who Were Brutally Killed

Jack Smith

Efforts have been made to ensure that the information in this book is accurate and complete. However, the author and the publisher do not warrant the accuracy of the information, text, and graphics contained within the book due to the rapidly changing nature of science, research, known and unknown facts, and the internet. The author and the publisher do not hold any responsibility for errors, omissions, or contrary interpretation of the subject matter herein. This book is presented solely for motivational and informational purposes only.

Warning
Throughout the book, there are some descriptions of murders and crime scenes that some people might find disturbing. There might be also some language used by people involved in the murders that may not be appropriate.

Note
Words in italic are quoted words from verbatim and have been reproduced as is, including any grammatical errors and misspelled words.

ISBN 9798763883565

Printed in the United States

Contents

Nothing to Celebrate

Much of the world is in the thrall of celebrity. Whether it's the big stars who stride across the big screen or reality TV characters whose lives are obsessively followed—it seems that people just can't get enough of celebrities. We lift celebrities up to incredible heights in our own imagination, yet we are so shocked if they happen to fall down from the pedestal upon which we place them.

If these larger-than-life characters fall victim to the darker side, it's always a stunning sight to see. Bob Crane, for example, was America's darling in the popular sitcom, "Hogan's Heroes." But after he turned up bludgeoned to death, a whole other side of Bob Crane emerged, one that included multiple orgy sessions, which he liked to capture on home video and in photographs.

It wasn't exactly unheard of for a celebrity to have a busy sex life, but Bob was one of the first to commit these escapades on tape. This salacious aspect of his life would make it very hard for subsequent investigators to focus on what actually killed him, after his brutal death. As much as Bob documented his high-rolling Hollywood lifestyle, another creep by the name of Victor Palaeologus was busy conning young women into thinking he was a big-time Hollywood photographer.

He claimed that one photo session with him would have them on the way to starring on the silver screen as "a Bond girl" in the latest James Bond movie. This was, of course, just a big fat lie, told in order for this Hollywood wannabe to procure girls he wished to take advantage of. But something went wrong in the middle of one of his scams and a young woman ended up dead.

Even though Victor was not really the Hollywood mogul he pretended to be, just the fact that he put forth this claim in the name of murder was enough to dim some of that Tinseltown shine. For when the worst of intentions and Hollywood mix, it's not exactly a good sight to behold. And despite the presence of celebrity—there's suddenly nothing to celebrate.

The Sudden Disdain of Bob Crane

Who*:* Bob Crane
Where: Scottsdale, Arizona
When: 1978
Suspect*:* John Carpenter/Unknown
Conviction*:* No Conviction/Unsolved

Background Information

Bob Crane was beloved for his role in the World War II sitcom, called "Hogan's Heroes." Although the humor involved was decidedly dark—Hogan and company were POWs at a Nazi prison—the show was surprisingly upbeat. The program aired decades after the end of World War II, and by then the horrors of the war were far enough in the rearview mirror, that an American audience felt comfortable enough to make light of them.

Every episode Hogan, played by Bob Crane, would help his fellow captives outsmart and play pranks on their bumbling Nazi guards. The show had a popular run for several seasons before going off the air in the early 1970s. Bob wasn't sure what else to do with his Hollywood career at that point until finally, he decided to tread the boards in theatrical productions.

Bob always enjoyed theatre and it was relaxing for him to escape the Hollywood lights and cameras for a bit, and perform for live audiences on stage. He found his footing in a popular production called "Beginner's Luck." Bob Crane had another hobby, however—videography. He had spent many years in front of the camera playing Hogan, but a later interest developed, being behind the camera.

He filmed all kinds of things, but what would be most startling in the aftermath of his murder was the revelation that he had a penchant for creating home sex tapes. He videotaped women in provocative poses, himself performing with these women, and on some occasions, he even had the camera going for full-blown orgies that involved him and several other people. It was while he was in the midst of all this, that Bob suddenly turned up dead.

On that Day

Victoria Ann Berry—Bob Crane's co-star from "Beginner's Luck" was the one who first happened upon the murder scene. She was concerned for Bob when he was a no show at the Television Academy luncheon that he was scheduled to attend with her, in which they were both scheduled to do an interview about the production. It wasn't like Bob to miss a chance for publicity, so Victoria thought she would head on over to his apartment herself to see what was up.

Upon arriving where Crane lived, she noticed that his vehicle was in the parking lot, so she assumed that he must be home. After knocking on the door, there wasn't any response. Frustrated, she gave the doorknob a try and discovered that it was unlocked.

Not sure of what else to do, she carefully made her way inside. Stepping in from the Arizona heat, she immediately felt the coolness of Bob's AC unit (a real luxury in the 1970s) which was continuously pumping cool air into the apartment.

She noticed stacks of magazines littering the floor and coffee table, and video and camera equipment were strewn throughout the living room. There was also a video camera set up on a tripod, pointed directly at the couch. This was no doubt where Bob recorded all of his infamous "home movies." As she made her way to Bob's bedroom, she noticed what she thought was someone sleeping on the bed on their right side, in the fetal position.

To her shock, Victoria then noticed that there was a "dark pool" of blood coming from the resting person's head. The blood was coming from Bob's left temple, and the carnage was so bad, that it obscured his face. Victoria wasn't sure if she was looking at Bob or perhaps his close friend John Carpenter, both of whom had a similar profile. As she looked closer, something did catch her eye—there appeared to be an electrical cord of some sort wrapped around the man's throat.

Whoever it was—this was no accident or mishap. This man did not fall and hit his head. This was quite obviously murder. Running out of the apartment, she flagged down the first person she could. She accosted a woman named Mary Lou Hawkins—the visiting mother of a resident—and requested her aid. Victoria pleaded with the startled Mary Lou, "Please help me, there's a man in the apartment who is dead, and I'm afraid it's Bob."

For a woman who spent her whole career working in the drama department, this was no doubt the most dramatic line that Victoria had ever uttered. It was Hawkins who got to a phone and called the Scottsdale Police Department to the scene. Upon the arrival of first responders, it was obvious that the bludgeoned man was dead, and nothing further could be done.

The body had yet to be identified, however, and Victoria insisted to officers on the scene that it could very well be Bob's friend John Carpenter who lay in bed, bludgeoned to death. This theory was dispelled however when John himself rang the phone at Bob's place and carried on a conversation with police officers on the scene. With Carpenter eliminated as a potential victim, it wouldn't take long for investigators to deduce that it was indeed Bob Carpenter who had been murdered.

The Investigation

Shortly after Bob Crane turned up dead, investigators went all over Crane's apartment building in an attempt to locate any potential witnesses. It was a busy apartment complex after all, and it was assumed that surely someone must have heard *something*. But as they went from unit to unit, they encountered residents who claimed to have not heard a single, solitary sound.

The only potential clue they received was from a resident named Sandy Miller, who claimed to have seen something that struck her as odd the previous night. She claimed to have seen Bob's car pull in, and to have seen Bob step out, followed closely by a "heavyset individual" whom she had never seen before. Who was this "heavyset individual?" A potential suspect?

Such details would indeed make investigators pause because the severity of Bob's injures led them to believe from the outset that whoever killed him must have been a "very strong man." The subsequent autopsy of Bob's body did indeed indicate that someone with plenty of brute force at their disposal had unleashed terror on Bob Crane. With this limited bit of a lead in mind, investigators fanned out to speak with Bob's friends and colleagues, to figure out just what his activities were like, off the set of "Beginners Luck."

They were in for an earful. It was then that the full range of Bob's prolific sex life became known. He had multiple partners at any given time, and much of it was documented on film. Investigators would leave Bob's residence with several bags full of Bob's home videos and photographs. Bob had videotaped so much of his time spent in that apartment, it was wondered if his own killing might somehow be on tape.

One of the early problems in the investigation, however, was a lack of control over the crime scene. Bob's adult son Bob Jr. for example, was allowed to come over almost immediately after the murder and was told he was free to take whatever he wanted. It's perhaps understandable that the police would want to show this kind of compassion to a loved one of a murder victim, but it flies in the face of the normal forensic protocol.

So, boxes of potential crime scene evidence were allowed to float right out of Bob Crane's apartment, never to be seen again. Another problem with the investigation was that many of the investigators just didn't take the case seriously. There were several accounts of guys on the scene goofing off watching Bob's sex tapes, rather than actually trying to solve his murder.

Police investigator Dean would recall sitting around with other investigators trying to discuss potential suspects when one of the guys irreverently shouted, "Put on the dirty movies!" Definitely not a good start for a serious investigation. Nevertheless, the early days of the investigation did yield some clues.

For one thing, the autopsy determined that the electrical cord around Bob's neck did not kill him. It seems that it was wrapped around his throat *after* he had already been bludgeoned to death—the reasoning behind this post mortem act remained a mystery. It was clear that the actual murder weapon must have been a heavy, solid steel object, in order to inflict the massive damage that it did.

The closest lead that investigators had on a suspect quickly became his close friend John Carpenter. No one, in fact, was quite as close as Carpenter when it came to Bob Crane. John Carpenter, in fact, was seen in many of Bob Crane's "home movies." Even more intriguing, it was discovered that Carpenter and Crane had actually been seen arguing the very day before Bob Crane's death.

Police subsequently got a warrant to search Carpenter's car. It was in the car that they found even more incriminating evidence—blood stains that appeared to belong to Bob Crane since they matched his blood type. It must be noted however that this was all that the forensics technology of the 1970s could yield. Beyond the actual blood type, investigators were unable to conclusively determine that the blood did indeed belong to Bob Crane.

The Suspect

Despite the lack of a smoking gun, once Bob Crane's blood type was discovered in his buddy John Carpenter's car,

Carpenter himself became a prime suspect. Initially, however, Arizona's Maricopa County DA wasn't interested in pursuing this lead, so amazingly enough, the case went cold. It wouldn't be picked up again until 1990 when a detective by the name of Barry Vassall took another look at the case and managed to convince the DA to give it another try.

Despite the years that had gone by, the new investigation uncovered something that the original investigators may have missed. There was an old crime scene photograph that Detective Vassall thought clearly depicted brain tissue inside Carpenter's car. Although perhaps a stab in the dark, this evidence was enough to bring John Carpenter in on charges of murder.

In the End

John Carpenter's trial began in 1994. During the course of the trial, Bob Crane's own son Bob Junior took the stand and testified that his father was sick of Carpenter mooching off of him and was just about to cut him off. It was Bob Crane Jr.'s understanding that Bob Crane Sr. had just ended his friendship with John Crane and Carpenter had killed him out of spite. Carpenter and his defense team refuted this, however, and presented statements from eyewitnesses that supposedly saw the two palling around together like best buds, the very day before the murder.

They also convincingly argued that the original investigation into Bob's death had been haphazard—claims that original investigators such as Dean could only confirm—and that the idea that brain tissue, that could not be tested, was found in a crime scene photo was ridiculed as absurd.

The defense also convincingly argued that Bob's killer could have been any number of boyfriends or husbands of the women he slept with, who might have killed the man out of revenge. John Carpenter was ultimately found not guilty by the jury, and he would insist upon his innocence until the day he died, in 1998.

Nevertheless, Maricopa County DA Rick Romley is still convinced that Carpenter was indeed the killer. As late as 2015, he went on the record to state, "I am convinced John Carpenter murdered Bob Crane." Once all is said and done, however, this case still remains officially unsolved.

Have a Heart for Phil Hartman

Who*:* Phil Hartman
Where: Hollywood, California
When: May 1998
Suspect*:* Brynn Hartman
Conviction*:* 1998 (suspect died before being convicted)

Background Information

Phil Hartman became famous on "Saturday Night Live," where his skits are now legendary. But as much as he is known for his life's work, he is also known for his disturbing death—shot three times by his own wife before she too took her own life. A native of Ontario, Canada, Phil was born on September 24th, 1948. His parents were of fairly modest means, and he and his brothers and sisters are said to have grown up in some fairly cramped conditions.

But eventually, his father was able to build two additional rooms onto the family homestead, thereby alleviating some of the strain. By the late 1950s, his family had made the decision to leave Canada behind, however, and moved down to the United States. Phil initially struggled to fit into community life outside the home, and inside the family, he felt unnoticed.

He came from a big family and his brother John tended to get all of the positive attention due to his good looks, athletic ability, and natural charisma. Phil soon discovered that the only way for him to stand out was to become as abrasive and obnoxious as possible. He would later credit this compulsion to cause himself to get noticed, as the ultimate drive that led him to become a comedian.

Growing up he was remembered as an A, B, and C student. Rarely would he get a D or an F, but he never tried hard enough academically to be on the honor roll either. Instead, his interest lay in the growing list of celebrities that he enjoyed impersonating. Rather than good grades, he was known around school for his hilarious takes on stars such as John Wayne, Bob Newhart, and Jonathan Winters.

It was Phil's spot-on impersonations that got him the attention of fellow student John Holloway, with whom he shared a homeroom class. As odd as they may have seemed to others, a favorite pastime of the pair was to go over to Holloway's house and watch old movies on mute so that they could insert their own parodied dialogue.

If you've ever seen the gag program "Mystery Science Theatre 3000" in which the narrators make remarks throughout cheesy films, then you basically get the idea of what these two goofy friends were up to.

But as strange as the pastime may have seemed to outsiders, it was actually stunts like this that served as preparation and dress rehearsal for a guy who would become one of the greatest sketch artists ever to appear on "Saturday Night Live".

Yes, by the time that he graduated from Westchester High School on June 17th, 1966, Phil knew that his true passion was somewhere outside of the halls of academia. Even so, upon his graduation, he made sure to sign up for classes at Santa Monica City College, where in between surfing with his buddies on the beach, he took some classes.

He eventually used his coursework at Santa Monica as a springboard to attend California State University, where Phil ended up graduating with a Bachelors's in Fine Art. Fresh out of school, he had some success with his artistic endeavors, and at one point designed artwork for the music group, America. He also married his first wife, Gretchen Lewis, around this time, before divorcing her in 1972.

By the mid-70s however, he needed to get back to his comedic roots and he hooked up with a local band of comedians that were dubbed "The Groundlings." Another famous member of this group was Paul Reubens, who would eventually develop the famous character of "Pee-wee Herman." Indeed, Phil Hartman would eventually come to make cameo appearances in the 1980's hit show "Pee-wee's Playhouse." Hartman stared as the absurd pirate— *Kap'n Karl.*

It was in the guise of this character that Phil Hartman sang his own personal theme song, "Oh, a sailor travels to many lands… Any place he pleases…. And he always remembers to wash his hands…. So's he don't get no diseases!" This role provided Hartman instant notoriety, but it was in 1986 when he was recruited to join the cast of "Saturday Night Live" (SNL) that Hartman's career really took off.

A lot of things happened in the meantime, Phil married his second wife, Lisa Strain in 1982, divorcing her in 1985. Hartman would remain on SNL for eight full seasons, before leaving the cast in 1994. He left behind several memorable skits including the infamous "Crosby Show" skit, mimicking the Cosby Show, complete with guest Jamal Warner (who played Theo on Cosby). During the act, instead of being Bill Cosby, Phil Hartman played 1940's crooner Bing Crosby!

But no doubt the most memorable moments of Phil Hartman's tenure at SNL was his "Unfrozen Caveman

Lawyer" routine, in which he played the part of a caveman who thawed out from the Ice Age, went to law school, and became a lawyer. In this role, Phil reprised the infamous catchphrase, "Ladies and gentlemen of the jury, I'm just a caveman... Your world frightens and confuses me..."

It was during his high flying run at SNL, that Phil Hartman married his third (and final) wife—Brynn Omdahl. The two got hitched on November 25th, 1987. Although happy that Phil had found someone, his friends noted from the beginning that Brynn was possessive and easily jealous of her husband.

Phil's ex-wife Lisa got a taste of this over-the-top jealous treatment herself when she sent Phil and Brynn a card congratulating the couple on their new child who was born in 1988. Although Lisa was no longer married to Phil, they were still friendly and on good terms, and it was simply something she did to wish both Phil—as well as his new wife Brynn—all the best.

Admittedly, there are a lot of people who might feel a little unsettled to receive any communication—even a nice congratulatory note—from the ex-spouse of their husband or wife. But as a celebrity, who hobnobbed with countless men and women on a regular basis, for Phil it was just part of the territory.

And regardless of how Brynn might have felt about it, her response was certainly in the extreme. After getting the congratulatory note, Brynn sent back a rage-filled letter to Lisa in which she basically threatened to kill her if she didn't stay away from Phil. In light of how things turned out, some might say that this was a red flag, warning everyone of things to come.

At any rate, after leaving SNL, Phil starred in a wide variety of small roles. The most famous of which was perhaps the most surprising. Phil was cast for some voice acting for a character on the animated series "The Simpsons." His first forays with the popular cartoon sitcom actually began before he left Saturday Night Live, and would become a recurring gig in Phil's later years.

In the show, he did the voice-over for a washed-up former actor named "Troy McClure." The character was partially based on some of Phil's own experiences of rejection and mid-life crisis as an actor. The humorous character was often shown appearing on the Simpson's television set during late-night infomercials, in which he always began with, "Hello—I'm Troy McClure, you might remember me from such films as…" before mentioning some absurd title to an obscure B-movie from decades gone by. The character, of course, was a total gag, but Troy McClure would go on to become a cult favorite in the Simpsons' universe.

At any rate, while Phil experimented with these amusing side gigs, no one was quite sure what Phil Hartman's next major project might be. Then came "News Radio" a sitcom that cast Phil as the overbearing radioman "Bill McNeal." The show would be fairly successful in its initial run, and the future once again looked promising. But all of these possibilities came to an end in 1998, when the unthinkable occurred.

On that Day

In the lead-up to Phil Hartman's death, he and his wife Brynn's relationship had deteriorated. This was due in large part to her worsening addiction to drugs and alcohol. The couple frequently fought over her substance abuse problems and on May 28th, 1998 one of those arguments took a deadly turn.

Early that morning, after a heated exchange, Brynn picked up a gun and shot Phil Hartman several times. After killing her husband, Brynn proceeded to drink and snort cocaine, before calling up her friend Douglas. Douglas gets a call from Brynn just after 3 in the morning. Bryn asks Douglas if she can come over to his house. Douglas tells her it's late, and she should probably stay home.

Around 4 in the morning Douglas is woken up to find Brynn banging on his door. Brynn, entirely intoxicated, burst into Douglas' home and began to rant and rave about killing Phil. Considering her state, Douglas didn't take her words seriously and figured it was just the booze talking.

Brynn eventually collapsed on the floor, only to wake up moments later, to run to the bathroom and throw up. At one point, however, Brynn produces a gun from her purse, which Douglas immediately takes from her. He examines the gun, and it initially appears that all six bullets are in the little six-shooter. Douglas is relieved, thinking that her ramblings about shooting Phil must be imaginary.

At a second glance, however, he realizes he is mistaken and sees that three of the bullets had indeed been expended. Growing concerned, he has Brynn drive back to her home, with his car following close behind so that he can check on Phil himself. Upon entering the residence, Douglas then learns the terrible truth. After seeing Phil's dead body stretched out on the bed—Douglas realizes that Brynn *did* indeed kill her husband, Phil Hartman.

The Investigation

Douglas called 911, upon finding Phil's body. With first responders on the way, Brynn suddenly ran into the bedroom where Phil lay and locked herself inside. She made one last frantic call out to her sister Kathy asking her to take care of her kids before Brynn picked up another gun (Phil was an avid gun collector—so there were several around) and shot herself.

Police broke through the locked doors of the bedroom shortly thereafter and found Brynn lying by her slain husband's side with a gun in hand. Since it was quite clear who the killer was, the investigation was concluded with Brynn's death.

The Suspects

Phil Hartman's wife Brynn appeared to be the obvious suspect. If the circumstances of her death had not been so obvious, however, one could imagine a few other suspects that would have potentially emerged. Douglas, for example, could have been turned into a suspect if investigators would have considered it possible that he had staged the whole thing himself.

Fortunately for Douglas however, Brynn's guilt was obvious. Brynn's manic spiral was documented not just by Douglas, but also through phone call conversations between Brynn and her sister Kathy, as well as dialogue recorded between her and emergency personnel. Police were then right on the scene just before Brynn killed herself, making all involved absolutely certain that Brynn was indeed the killer.

In the End

There was no conviction since Brynn took her own life the very same day she killed Phil Hartman, in 1998.

Denise Huber
Hunted in Hollywood

Who*:* Denise Huber
Where: Hollywood, California
When: June 1991
Suspect*:* John Famalaro
Conviction*:* 1997

Background Information

Denise Huber was born on November 22nd, 1967, and was only 23 years old when she went missing after attending a Morrissey concert in Hollywood. A California native, she and her younger brother Jeff were raised by her father Dennis and their mother Ione, in the greater Los Angeles area. She was still living with her parents at the time of her disappearance but was nevertheless fiercely independent.

So independent in fact, that she would often come and go as she pleased, without her or her parents giving it much of a second thought. She had even gone with a family friend to London on one occasion and everything turned out just fine. So, when she failed to return from that Morrissey concert in 1991, her parents initially told themselves not to worry.

She had gone to the concert with her buddy Rob Calvert. Rob was just a friend, and Denise had many guy friends.

Her male buddies no doubt found her attractive, with her perfect figure, long brown hair, and bright blue eyes. But Denise at this point in her life wasn't looking for a serious relationship, she was just looking to enjoy life in the company of friends.

Initially, she was to attend the concert with another male friend—Jason Snyder—but he had to bail out on those plans when he found out he couldn't get off work. Denise first met Jason at the Old Spaghetti Factory where they had both worked together, and as a past employee, she certainly understood how busy the place could get.

But she still wanted someone to go to the concert with her. It was Jason who suggested that their mutual friend—and one-time co-worker—Rob could join her for the show in his place. Rob didn't drive at the time, so it was, of course, Denise who would provide the transportation with her snazzy blue, 1988 Honda. According to Rob's later testimony, Denise arrived right on time and took him to the concert which was located at the Forum in the vicinity of the Hollywood Park race track.

He recalled having a great time with Denise and although the two had a few drinks, he insisted that it was not in excess. They were able to let loose with the crowd however once Morrissey took the stage. Rob especially recalled how they had joyfully chanted out the artist's name "Morrissey!! Morrissey!! Morrissey!" as he performed his hit song "[I'm] The End of My Family Line."

They were having so much fun, that Rob even managed to put his arm around his otherwise physically skittish friend, while they soaked in the intensity of the performance. According to Rob's testimony, after the concert, Denise stepped over to a nearby payphone (this was many years before cellphones of course) and called up their buddy Jason Snyder, since he had by then finished work.

She invited Jason to meet up with her and Rob at a local Mexican diner called the El Paso Cantina so that they could all three hang out. Rob recalled the roads being clogged with traffic as they made their way to the exit ramp for California's I-405 Interstate Highway. Nevertheless, Denise managed to maneuver her Honda well enough, and they arrived at the El Paso Cantina as planned.

Here they had a couple of drinks and listened to music on the restaurant's jukebox and waited for Jason Snyder to arrive. Jason ultimately wasn't able to make it, however, and by the time that the restaurant's bar gave their last call for alcohol, Denise and Rob decided that they better head out. Rob would later recall just one more stop before getting back to his house—at a convenience store to get some cigarettes.

The last time Rob saw Denise was right after she parked in front of his house to drop him off. Rob would recall how his seatbelt had jammed and he struggled to unbuckle it. Denise then reached over and managed to free her passenger. The two then talked and laughed for a few more minutes, before Rob bid his friend farewell.

Denise's parents knew Rob Calvert fairly well and considered him an honest, trustworthy young man. They were sure he would serve as a good company—and if need be—protection for their daughter. Even if Denise had decided to crash at Rob's house after the concert, they wouldn't have given it a second thought.

It was Only after Denise's mom called Rob the following morning to find that she wasn't there, that the family started to get concerned. Rob, in fact, was positive that Denise said that she was heading straight home to her parents' house, immediately after she dropped him off in the wee hours of the morning. Yet Denise never arrived. It would be a panicked, full 24 hours later that her abandoned car would be discovered on the side of the road.

The Disappearance

In the aftermath of Denise Huber's disappearance, investigators spoke to several of her friends in order to get a better idea of both Denise, and the potential circumstances of how she could have gone missing. Rob Calvert, being the last person to see her prior to her disappearance, was of course of immediate interest. And so was Jason Snyder, the co-worker with whom she had initially intended to attend the concert.

Another source of information, however, came by way of Denise's good friend Tammy. Tammy had hung out with Denise for some time. She had attended previous concerts with her, such as David Bowie in May, and a Depeche Mode concert in August. The Depeche Mode concert in particular was a memorable affair for Tammy. For whatever reason, the synth-pop/rock group was slow to come on stage.

Anxious fans growing weary of waiting began to grow distressed. Then when some trouble makers on the upper level decided to pour their drinks on people down below— all hell broke loose. It was at that very moment that Depeche Mode waltzed out onto the stage. Tammy could recall the bizarre spectacle of rioting fans as the vocalist for Depeche Mode crooned the words to their 1980's hit, "Everything Counts" in perfect harmony.

As concertgoers pushed and shoved each other, vocalist David Gahan belted out the chorus, "The grabbing hands, grab all that they can…. All for themselves… After all….. The grabbing hands grab all that they can….. All for themselves….. After all…."

It was one night among many, that Tammy would not forget. Tammy knew that Denise loved concerts, and she was also well aware of the Morrissey concert that Denise had attended right before her disappearance. Tammy remembered her time spent with her friend well, and she would be of key importance as the investigation into Denise's disappearance began.

The Investigation Leads to the Body

Denise's parents Dennis and Ione were growing increasingly worried after their daughter failed to come home on the morning of June 3rd, 1991. Initially, they tried to rationalize that perhaps she had crashed at a friend's house—that wouldn't have been uncommon for their daughter. But a few phones calls later to the friends she most likely would have been in contact with—and it became clear that this was not the case.

Shortly after her disappearance, Denise's abandoned Honda was then found on the side of the road with a flat tire. It was actually found by Denise's friend Tammy Brown. Tammy, just as desperate for answers as Denise's parents, attempted to retrace the route Denise would have followed, and sure enough, she saw the blue Honda parked and deserted on the shoulder of the busy freeway.

Tammy had been called by Denise's mother the morning of her disappearance, to see if she knew where Denise might be. Concerned for her friend, Tammy decided to drive around herself to look for her. Upon seeing the abandoned vehicle with Denise nowhere in sight, Tammy recalled having a terrible "sinking feeling" in her stomach, as she cried out to herself, "Oh my God—Denise where are you?"

Immediately after this dreadful discovery, a panicked Tammy exited off the highway and found a payphone at a nearby convenience store, and called up Denise's Mom and Dad to let them know what she had discovered. Denise's parents were then summoned to the scene, and finding the vehicle unlocked with Denise's keys inside, they confirmed that it was indeed Denise's Honda.

But with Denise nowhere in sight and unsure what else they could do—Denise's worried parents decided to head home so that they could call the police. What a difference a cellphone makes, right? Today if something like this had happened, the worried parents would have called the cops as soon as they got to the scene. But since Denise's parents didn't have the luxury of a cellphone, they had to hustle on back to their home just to call 911.

Once home, Dennis picked up the old landline phone and dialed up the Newport Beach Police Department. After filling in the police with the details, they were instructed to call a tow truck to get the car, and to then file a missing person's report for Denise. Even the very words, "missing person report" must have made these worried parents tremble at the thought.

It's a horrible uncertainty to go through, to have a loved one missing, with no idea of where they are and who they might be with. And the very act of having to file a "missing person's report" only confirms the awful terror that this situation instills. It was shortly after these efforts were made that the police officers converged to the site of Denise's abandoned Honda.

Upon arriving at the scene, investigators deduced the obvious, that Denise was not in the vehicle. They then fanned out with flashlights to scan the immediate vicinity, to see if there was any further sign of Denise, or at least what might have befallen her. Another police officer—Jane Walker—was on the scene with a dog from the K9 unit. She walked this dog around the car to see if it could pick up a scent. The dog almost immediately seemed to do so.

The dog yanked his handler some 75 feet in front of the Honda. Here the K9 came to a rest and turned back to Jane as if to tell her that this was the last trace of Denise that was to be found. The dog seemed to indicate that Denise had walked or was forcibly moved, some 75 feet from the car, and then the trail went cold. Now either Denise instantly teleported from that spot, or the trail ceased because she entered a vehicle. It was quite obvious that a car must have parked some 75 feet in front of Denise's distressed vehicle, and Denise either willingly or by coercion was taken from the scene by the other motorist.

Nevertheless, despite this indication, the police continued to search the area, just in case Denise might be found. After this first routine search was completed, the car was towed to a "police storage yard" since the car itself was now evidence of a potential crime. As the investigation began to heat up, a seasoned police detective—Ron Smith—began work on the case. Smith started with first things first. Why did Denise get a flat tire? The most obvious answer would be that the tire had simply blown out and gone flat on its own. A common enough occurrence, especially if the tire happened to be poorly inflated.

But Smith wished to rule out any chance that someone somewhere may have purposefully damaged her tire beforehand. Could a sinister concert-goer back at the Forum have tampered with Denise's tire? Smith wanted to find out, so he had a group of experts examine the flat tire. Upon examination, however, the examiners concluded that the tire had not been tampered with. Considering that Denise had gotten a flat on her own without any outside tampering, the next question on this investigator's mind was what Denise might have done in such a situation.

Besides pulling over to the side of the road and turning her flashers on—as she obviously had done—Smith figured she would probably try to find a phone so that she could dial someone up for assistance. Once again, since this was the early 1990s Denise did not have the luxury of having a cellphone right there in her vehicle, so she would have had to have walked to a payphone or emergency call box.

This puzzled Smith, however, because there was indeed an emergency call box not far from Denise's car. A short walk would have brought her to the call box, where she could have summoned aid. Denise could have also easily walked off the freeway to a nearby payphone. Yet, apparently, this is not what Denise decided to do that night. Then again, the K9 who sniffed her trail, indicated that she did walk about 75 feet from her car in the direction of payphones. Could it be that this young woman was intercepted on her way to the call box?

This was, of course, the greatest fear of Denise's friends and family. And for the man who had skipped out on the concert that night—Jason Snyder—these fears were particularly acute. He knew Denise well enough to know that she wouldn't just take rides from strangers, for him it was pretty clear that she must have been abducted by someone. His only hope at this point was that she was still alive somewhere, and could be rescued. He realized the chances were slim, but Snyder joined forces with investigators in the search for answers.

Jason Snyder posted thousands of flyers all over California. He hoped that someone who knew something would come forward so that they could find Denise. And soon enough, someone did come forward. But not to say that they had seen Denise, but rather her Honda. This was important because of the time in which this witness had seen the vehicle. The eyewitness was a woman named Cynthia Brown who delivered papers in the early morning hours, and it was not at all uncommon for her to be on the highway, headed toward her routes around 2 or 3 in the morning.

And during these early morning twilight hours of June 3rd, when Denise went missing, she vividly recalled seeing a blue Honda parked on the side of the highway with its emergency lights flashing. She guessed the time was just after 2 in the morning. This was important because this would have been shortly after Denise would have left her friend Rob's house, and been on her way home.

These details seemed to perfectly corroborate the idea that Denise had indeed got a flat shortly after dropping off Rob Calvert. Considering the timing, detectives were hopeful that perhaps Cynthia could provide some further clues. So, they asked her the obvious—did she see a young woman matching Denise's description at the scene? But Cynthia had not. Nor had she seen any suspicious character lurking in the shadows.

Nevertheless, her testimony was crucial because it established that the flat tire must have occurred right after Denise had dropped off Rob. But it was shortly after this one lone clue, that this case would begin to grow cold. No further progress would be made for three whole years.

Yes, it was in the summer of 1994, about three years after Denise first went missing, that yet another keen eye witness just happened to notice something unusual that got her attention.

Elaine Canalia had been dealing with a paint contractor, by the name of John Famalaro and at one point was at his house getting some paint for a project, when she noticed something she felt was altogether unusual. A yellow Ryder rental truck was backed into the painter's driveway. The truck was partially obscured by a piece of tarp and was surrounded by stacked cans of paint, almost as if they were meant to serve as a barricade, preventing access to the truck.

The whole thing was strange, it was obvious that the truck had not been in use for a while, yet there it sat taking up space. The painter also raised eyebrows when he refused to allow Elaine's 10-year-old grandson who had accompanied her, to use the bathroom. John Famalaro claimed the water was turned off, but to her, it seemed like an excuse to simply not allow them to see the inside of his house.

Nevertheless, Famalaro led them behind his house and grabbed some paint cans, which he helped load into their vehicle. Elaine thanked the man for the paint and left. But the strange experience would stick with her. She was so disturbed by it in fact, that she made herself memorize the license plate of the truck while she was in the man's yard— just in case it might prove useful later on. And it sure did.

Shortly thereafter she mentioned the experience to a friend of hers who happened to be a police detective—Steve Gregory. Gregory wasn't necessarily thinking that the truck might have something to do with a missing person at the time, but he did consider the fact that it might be stolen. It was unusual, after all, for a citizen to just happen to have a Ryder rental truck permanently parked at their home.

Detective Gregory checked with the rental company and found that it had indeed been stolen from them. He then ran the plates thanks to Elaine's description, and an officer—Deputy Joe DiGiacomo—was sent to check on the lead, and went to the painter's house. John Famalaro had since changed the plate, however, and after the officer approached on foot and made this discovery, it sent him scrambling back to have to double-check his sources.

DiGiacomo returned with another cop, Detective Garcia, for support, and this time they were able to look at the VIN number. This proved a match. Regardless of the switched plates, the VIN number indicated that this was indeed the same vehicle. They also noticed something puzzling: there was a long extension cord under the sealed, sliding rear door. The cord stretched all the way into the house as if plugged into a power source.

Confronted with this strange sight, the detectives on the scene weren't thinking of missing persons and murder, but what they did consider was that perhaps this cord was powering some sort of mobile drug lab within the truck. Knowing that these sorts of arrangements were not only illegal but highly dangerous, since meth labs were prone to sudden explosions, the detectives decided to immediately try to get in contact with the homeowner.

After repeated knocks, however, no one ever came to the door. The police then contacted the narcotics squad, who came on the scene shortly thereafter. They also had a locksmith come to the scene, and in a short time, they had the truck open and were able to go inside. It was in the back of the truck that they found what the extension cord was plugged into—a large refrigerator/freezer.

The freezer was the kind someone might store meat in, with one big, single door on top of the unit. The fridge like everything else was also surrounded by paint cans. It was also curiously wrapped in what looked like masking tape.

The detectives cut the tape off, and quite literally holding their breath, opened up the freezer. They, in fact, needed to hold their breath, because a terrible smell was emitted as soon as the freezer was open.

At first glance, they still weren't sure what was causing the smell, since the contents of the freezer were covered by a bunch of black trash bags. Detective Garcia bravely put a gloved hand down on top of the trash bags, however, and pressed into them. He was startled to feel what seemed to take the shape of a person's appendage.

It was once they determined that they had a frozen dead body on their hands, that the detectives ceased their investigation lest they disturb evidence, and called in a professional homicide unit. It was indeed a horrific sight to behold. The suspect, John Famalaro in the meantime, had finally been caught up with, arrested on July 13th, right in front of his home.

The Suspect

John Famalaro was arrested on charges of felony theft for the stealing of a Ryder rental truck on July 13th, 1994. This was just the first of many charges to come. The professional homicide team uncovered the body of a deceased young woman, with her hands handcuffed behind her back, frozen in a fetal position in the freezer. And although John himself wasn't talking, his home was being searched and several incriminating items would be uncovered.

They found a "nail bar" and a "claw hammer" with blood on them, which immediately stood out as potential murder weapons. They also found handcuffs identical to the pair found on the dead body, along with handcuff keys. But most damning of all, they retrieved a black bag that had pieces of identification with Denise Huber's name on them.

It was now abundantly clear that Denise had been found, and the main suspect in her killing was in police custody. Denise's parents were immediately notified. They were deeply saddened, as would be expected, but were at least finally able to stop wondering what had happened to their daughter.

The suspected killer John Famalaro on the other hand had a family that claimed to have no knowledge of what John was up to. Disturbingly enough, however, it would later be discovered that John's own mother had tried her hand at murder in the past. John's older brother George had been seeing a woman named Velma many years prior—a woman that John and George's mother did not appear to like.

Mrs. Famalaro had tracked the woman down to a hotel, barged in the room, leaped upon her, and attempted to choke the young lady to death. Velma however, was, fortunately, able to fight the older lady off and escape her clutches. This certainly was a serious crime, but Mrs. Famalaro managed to escape prosecution, since Velma ultimately didn't press charges at the insistence of her boyfriend, George.

The idea that John Famalaro's own mother was capable of such extreme violence, only added to the disturbing profile being built for John Famalaro himself. At the time of Denise's murder, John was a quiet, loner in his late 30s. But John, just like his mother, had an explosive temper. It would be the contention of the prosecution at John's trial that it was this rage that was unleashed on Denise, when John bludgeoned her to death, shattering her skull with a hammer.

Trial and Conviction

Initially, you might think that someone like John Famalaro, who was found to have a dead body in a stolen rental truck, would be a slam dunk case for the prosecution. But at the outset of his trial, establishing a guilty verdict was not as easy as it might seem. Everyone tried by the justice system, after all, is supposed to be considered innocent until proven guilty. And since John wasn't about to confess to murder, the burden of proving that guilt fell onto the prosecution.

John's defense team, on the other hand, did whatever they could to diminish John's perceived guilt. Sure—he had a dead body in a freezer in a rental truck. Sounds terrible—yet these legal spin doctors found ways to obscure the facts. First of all, they fought to have kidnapping charges dropped. They maintained that there was no evidence that John had forced Denise to go with him.

Even the prosecution acknowledged this fact and was split as to whether or not Denise was forced to go with John, or perhaps she was tricked into accepting a ride with him. John, after all, could have been posing as a good Samaritan and tricked Denise into getting into his vehicle by way of deceit rather than force. But the prosecution would come up with some pretty good circumstantial evidence to indicate that John was not above forcing ladies to do things against their will.

This came by testimony from former girlfriends of Famalaro who described his previous aggressive behavior. Two of them in fact described instances in which John surprised them during intimate moments, by suddenly slapping handcuffs on them. At the time, John had tried to laugh off the deviant behavior as just "sex games" but his former lovers were not amused. Both had even considered filing charges but eventually changed their minds.

Now, however, they were both front and center with their own personal testimony, indicating that Denise Huber most certainly wouldn't have been the first person to have cuffs slapped on her wrists by John Famalaro. More troubling for the Huber family was the issue of semen found in Denise's rectum. Even though this bodily fluid was detected, forensic technology was apparently not good enough—or the evidence was just too degraded at the time—to ascertain who the semen came from.

This led John's defense team to try to raise doubts as to whether or not the semen was from John. They insisted that although it was discovered that semen was in Denise's rectum, there was no clear indication as to who it was from. The defense, therefore, argued that it could have come from any other male that Denise was aquatinted with prior to her death, and not necessarily from their client, John Famalaro.

Having to sit through what seemed like the character assassination of their daughter, the Huber family was both enraged and mortified. Anyone who knew Denise understood that such things did not fit in with her lifestyle. Yes, she had many guy friends, but every single one would testify that Denise was just looking for friendship, and was not intimately involved with any of them.

Her parents knew this fact well, and so the mere suggestion of Denise being promiscuous before her death was galling in the extreme. One new piece of evidence that reignited the charge of kidnapping was the demonstration that Denise's shoes were damaged, and possibly indicated that she had been dragged off the highway and into John's vehicle.

In closing arguments, lead prosecutor Chris Evans pursued this angle and went at length to indicate that Denise was on her way to one of the nearby payphones or emergency call boxes when she was interrupted by Famalaro. Evans insisted that there was no reason for her to go with John

Famalaro since a quick walk to a call box or payphone would have got this stranded motorist all the help she needed.

According to Evans, the only reason Denise went with John was that she was forced to do so. This creep saw the flashing emergency lights of her vehicle, and rather than prompting him to render aid, this beacon of distress was his cue to prey upon the vulnerable. John then swooped down on Denise like a predatory vulture and forced her into his vehicle.

Or as Evans described it to the jury, "Ladies and gentlemen, Denise Huber did not go voluntarily past all this help. That didn't happen, not in this case, not in this lifetime, not on this planet. This is an area that she was intimately familiar with. This triangle of UCI where she went to college, her house, the location of the car, and Rob Calvert's house. She didn't go past all those convenience stores, payphones, all those lit areas. She didn't go past her college campus, not knowing where the heck she was."

These arguments were very persuasive to the jury, and ultimately John was indeed convicted of kidnapping, as well as murder, and in the Fall of 1997, he was sentenced to death for his crimes. He remains on death row at California's San Quentin Penitentiary to this very day.

Who was Chasing Ronni Chasen?

Who*:* Ronni Chasen
Where: Beverly Hills, California
When: November 2010
Suspect*:* Harold Martin Smith
Conviction*:* 2010 (Died)

Background Information

Ronni Chasen was born on October 17th, 1946, in Kingston, New York. She grew up in the Bronx, where her earliest brush with fame was through winning competitive yo-yo contests as a child. The yo-yo, of course, was a toy that was popular in the 1950s and 1960s, which consisted of a plastic, circular object on a string, which one could toss up and down as it unfurled from its yo-yo string. Yes, little Ronni apparently had quite a knack for the yo-yo.

But yo-yo's aside, her career as a budding publicist led her to Hollywood, where Ronni Chasen began to chase the stars on a regular basis, as a highly successful Hollywood publicist. She had success early on, promoting popular films such as "On Golden Pond," and "Driving Miss Daisy."

This success led to her being made Senior Vice President for Publicity for MGM. She also started her own agency called Chasen & Co. to promote talent. In 2010 she was avidly promoting "Alice in Wonderland". All of her work came to an abrupt end, however, on November 16th, 2010 when she was callously shot and killed while driving home from a Hollywood promotional event.

On that Day

Shortly after midnight on November 16th, 2010, Chasen was on her way back from "Burlesque", which was premiered in Hollywood at the time. She was passing through Beverly Hills when she was shot while cruising down Sunset Boulevard. Losing control of the car, Chasen crashed into a nearby street light. Police arrived on the scene to find her only semi-conscious. She was then rushed off to Cedars-Sinai Medical Center where she died upon arrival to the hospital.

The Investigation

The major piece of evidence for investigators to zero in on, after Roni Chasen was killed, was her bloody, and bullet-impacted vehicle. Investigators noted that Roni Chasen's passenger side window was shattered, indicating that she was shot by someone who was positioned on that side of her vehicle as she passed by. This caused her to crash just as she was attempting to swing onto Whittier Drive, at the intersection of Sunset Boulevard and Whittier.

Police felt that whoever shot out Chasen's window was someone who had pulled up right next to the car and fired at close range. This was an important clue because it ruled out the chance that Roni was hit by the crossfire of a random bullet. Although Hollywood is not exactly known for gang activity, it wouldn't be unheard of for gunfire to suddenly erupt between gangsters on opposite sides of a street, causing an innocent motorist to be caught in the crossfire.

But the damage to Roni's passenger side window seemed to indicate otherwise. It appeared that whoever shot out the window, had pulled up right next to her car and purposefully shot right inside at close range. This led investigators to consider very carefully, who might have wanted to harm this popular Hollywood publicist.

The Suspect

Shortly after her death, and at the very start of the investigation, it was reported by the media that Ronni Chasen's killer had been cornered by police and killed himself at his residence in East Hollywood. Police later confirmed that the suspected killer—a guy named Harold Martin Smith—was dead.

Police suspected that the killing was simply an attempted robbery gone bad. It has been speculated that Mr. Smith may have pulled up next to Ronni Chasen's car, pointed a gun at her, and demanded money. What might have happened next is pure speculation—but perhaps Ms. Chasen reached for her phone, or simply tried to get away and hit the accelerator to leave the bandit behind. Maybe the aggravated crook then took his rage out on her, by firing his weapon into her passenger side window.

Despite the tragic outcome, Ms. Chasen probably did the best thing she could considering the circumstances. There are many people after all, who have been in similar situations in which they had a gun pulled on them at a red light, and complied with the assailant, only to be carjacked, raped, robbed, and murdered, despite their cooperation.

If she saw a gun pointed at her and her instinct was to hit the gas and getaway, it was probably the best thing she could have done at the time. If this is indeed what transpired, it's just a shame that her assailant managed to fire off a shot before she was able to clear the intersection.

In the End

There was no trial or conviction in this case since the prime suspect took his own life in the middle of a standoff with police.

Myra Davis
The Body Double

Who*:* Myra Davis
Where: Hollywood, California
When: 1988
Suspect*:* Kenneth Hunt
Conviction*:* 2001

Background Information

In her later years as an actress, Myra Davis, played only small roles—often starring in commercials as what has been described as her being cast as the "quintessential grandmother." Innocent, unassuming, and loveable, were the traits that came to mind when Myra appeared on the screen. At this point, her heyday had passed, but in her youth, she had taken part in an Alfred Hitchcock classic.

The Hollywood thriller "Psycho" is a classic 1960s horror film that starred actress Janet Leigh, who played the victim of the movie's psychotic centerpiece—Norman Bates, played by Anthony Perkins. A woman called Myra Davis performed as Janet Leigh's body double during filming, and it was actually Myra who was seen in the infamous shower scene in the movie when Norman Bates lunges his knife at his unsuspecting victim.

Her role here, was quite controversial for the time since she appeared without clothes. Those that worked on set, however, were quick to point out that she wasn't entirely without wardrobe, as there were "patches of plaster" developed by the makeup artists which Myra wore to obscure the most intimate parts of her body. Nevertheless, for the 1960s this was some shocking stuff, even for her fellow actors.

Hitchcock is said to have used a closed set for the film, but that didn't keep some curious stagehands from sneaking on set to observe Myra for themselves. Nevertheless, Myra was comfortable with the role she played, and she always remembered Mr. Hitchcock—despite his reputation—as being a sweet and kind man who would do anything to put her at ease.

It seems such overtures were only right, considering the potentially awkward and stressful task that Myra was performing. Besides being nearly nude, she also had to act out her own death. And a death which occurred in a particularly brutal and bloody fashion. At any rate, filming finished up without a hitch (pun intended Hitchcock fans) and became the "Psycho" cinema classic we know today.

Bizarrely enough, this woman who stood in to get stabbed for actress Janet Leigh, was targeted and killed by her own real-life psycho—a deranged maintenance man by the name of Kenneth Hunt. This slaying occurred on March 28th, 1988 several decades after Myra worked on the set of "Psycho". She was 71 years old at the time, and it would take investigators many years to find the creep who seemed to get a thrill out of stalking older women.

On That Day

It was on July 3rd, 1988 that Sherry Davis paid her grandmother Myra Davis a visit. Just prior to her visit, she was notified by her uncle that Myra hadn't been answering the phone. It was then that Sherry volunteered to check on the older woman. It was indeed unusual for Myra to not answer the phone and if she wasn't home, it was odd that she wouldn't let anyone know that she was about to be gone for a long stretch of time. She almost always told a family member when she was going out, yet this time no one had any idea of where she might be.

Sherry let her husband John know that she was making the trip, and he was worried enough about the situation to suggest that he should escort her there. Shoving aside any trepidation however, Sherry insisted that she would go alone. As soon as she pulled up to her grandmother's house however, she felt that something was wrong. Her first indication was the fact that several newspapers were piled up on Myra's porch.

Myra always picked up the daily papers as soon as they arrived, and normally, she would never let them stack up like that. Yet, the papers were stacked up as if Myra had not been outside in several days. This alone, tipped Sherry off that Myra was in some kind of trouble.

By now Sherry was getting frightened, and no doubt wishing she had taken her husband up on his offer to accompany her. Not knowing what was going on—she was too scared to go inside, so she went around the back of the house and looked through a window. It was through a crack

47

in the blinds that she was able to see her grandmother Myra stretched out on her bed. And it was quite obvious that she was dead.

The Investigation

Realizing that her grandmother was dead, Sherry Davis hopped into her car and headed back home to enlist the aid of her husband. They called 911, and the couple then went back to the home and waited outside while they let the emergency responders go into the residence, to take care of the body. This was partially done out of respect since Myra's corpse was semi-nude, and neither Sherry nor her husband wished to see her in such a condition.

In the meantime, murder investigator—detective Gary Fullerton—made his way to the crime scene. Fullerton very quickly realized that Sherry had not only been murdered but had most likely been sexually assaulted.

This was obvious since she was nude from the waist down, and even the blouse that partially covered her had a white bra underneath that seemed to have been purposefully shoved aside, to reveal her breasts.

Or as Fullerton put in his actual report, "She was nude from the waist down. Her blouse had been pulled up and her bra opened." As distressing as all this was, maggots were also detected in the victim's mouth and nose, clearly indicating that the body had been there for a while. At least long enough for an errant fly or two to drop its payload of maggot eggs into her dead body.

Beyond Myra's body, the home, in general, had signs of disturbance. The drawers of her dresser were hanging out, and a nightstand looked as if it was sifted through as well. After a rape kit was used to collect samples, Myra's body was removed from the scene to be taken to a facility where a proper autopsy could be carried out.

Both the autopsy and the samples taken from the rape kit used on the scene confirmed that Myra had been sexually assaulted. Sherry's husband John was informed of these developments, but he initially withheld the details about the sexual assault, to shield his wife from further grief. It was Sherry, however, who tipped off investigators as to who she thought the suspect might be.

The Suspects

Call it a stab in the dark, or pure and simple neighborly suspicion, but the first person that Sherry thought might have harmed her grandmother was her next-door neighbor George Green. And she told police as much. She informed investigators that she suspected Green simply because of previous odd and creepy behavior. She claimed that he stared at her whenever she came over to her grandmother's home.

She did yard work for her grandmother sometimes, and Sherry claimed that she caught George ogling her as she worked in the yard. She also mentioned that he was known to just pop up at Myra's door uninvited and often made her grandmother feel uncomfortable as well. Police followed up this lead and questioned the next-door neighbors. George lived with nine other family members, so it took the investigators a while to sort through the others and get to George.

They did though, and after speaking with him and everyone else, they decided to dismiss George and his whole family as potential suspects. They all had alibis that seemed to check out. Interestingly enough, Sherry's pointing the finger at her grandmother's neighbors only seemed to accomplish getting the finger pointed right back at her own family.

For it was after speaking with the neighbors that Shelly disliked so much, that police learned that Shelly's older brother Corey was seen at the residence right before Myra's death, and also that he had a friend who had been working as a handyman for Myra during the preceding three weeks. After police detective Fullerton began questioning Shelly about her brother, it became obvious to her that her own family member was being made into a suspect.

She protested against this at the time, but the detective reminded her that eliminating a list of potential suspects was all part of the job, and now he was trying to eliminate the possibility that her brother Corey was a suspect. He also reminded her that although folks don't like to think about it—more often than not—as he put it, "people kill members of their own family."

The only thing that made Sherry wonder if her brother Corey was involved, was the fact that he had a bad drug habit, and she knew that he might not be above stealing to sustain it. Thinking of the rifled drawers, and stolen valuables, it wouldn't be hard to imagine Corey robbing his grandma so that he could sell stolen items for drug money. But beyond stealing, she didn't think that Corey would have physically harmed his grandmother. But then again, what if he had an accomplice?

This was one of the angles that investigators were pursuing, early on in this case. They theorized that perhaps it was a robbery gone wrong led by Corey, and it was his accomplice that brutalized the old lady. All of these suspicions wreaked havoc with Myra's relatives. Especially between Myra's two sons, with one pointing the finger at the other, for the suspected involvement of their own child.

Or as Sherry, herself put it, "Myra's other son, my uncle, was furious with my father. He blamed him for Corey's very existence and his substance abuse." It's pretty rough for one sibling to blame another for their own child's "very existence."

Eventually, however, all of this rancor would prove misplaced, and Corey would be eliminated as a suspect. But if it wasn't Corey who killed Myra—then who was it?

New developments in the case would eventually turn the detectives' attention back to Myra's neighbors. But it wasn't George Green who was the suspect, but rather George's brother-in-law Kenneth Hunt. Mr. Hunt, better known by his nickname "Sonny" had married Betty, the daughter of the matriarch of the household Doris Green.

Doris had nothing but good things to say about Sonny, whom she said cared for her and helped out around the house. But Sonny had a dark side. He was an ex-con who had already been convicted of various assault charges. And soon the evidence appeared to line up to suggest that Sonny had killed Myra.

Ten years after Myra's death another older woman in the neighborhood—Jeanine Orloff was killed under similar circumstances. Initially, however, when the elderly woman was found dead, it was assumed that she had suffered a heart attack. She was about to be cremated when a sharp-eyed coroner at the mortuary realized that her death was not a natural one—and concluded she had been murdered.

Although thankful for the coroner who ultimately made this realization, Orloff's family was frustrated at the initial confusion over Ms. Orloff's death. Or as Jeanine Orloff's sister Lois Bachrach, put it, "I find it appalling that so many mistakes can be made and no one has ever had to explain themselves."

At any rate, it was when it was discovered that Kenneth Hunt had been doing odd jobs at Jeanine Orloff's home at the time of her death, that he suddenly became a number one suspect. And with his suspicion of murder, in this case, it wasn't' t long before the murder of Myra Davis was re-opened as well. Soon it was quite clear to investigators that it was Kenneth "Sonny" Hunt who was involved in Myra's murder as well. Now they just had to prove it in court.

In the End

The most convincing piece of evidence linking Kenneth Hunt to the murder of Myra as well as Jeanine Orloff was DNA evidence collected by the forensics lab. These samples matched bloodwork taken from Kenneth Hunt. And it was this information that led to Kenneth's arrest. Kenneth Hunt stood trial for both Myra and Jeanine Orloff's murders in 2001. Kenneth was found guilty as charged and sentenced to life in prison without the possibility of parole.

George Reeves
Did the Man of Steel Self-Destruct?

Who: George Reeves
Where: Hollywood, California
When: 1959
Suspects: Eddie Mannix and Toni Mannix
Conviction: No Conviction

Background Information

George Reeves came into this world on the 5th of January, in 1914. Prior to adopting his "Hollywood name" of Reeves, he was known as George Keefer Brewer. George was born about as far removed from the glitz and glamour of Hollywood as one could be, in the rural trappings of Woolstock, Iowa. His parents split shortly after his birth, and his newly divorced mother packed up George and moved him off to Galesburg, Illinois.

Their life there would only last a few years, however, before George's mother, Helen decided to head to California. It was here that she ended up marrying a guy named Frank Joseph Besselo in 1920. George, therefore, became Frank's stepson and was thereafter called George Bessolo. George took to California life well enough and actively participated in theatre at school. Helen in the meantime ended up divorcing Frank some 15 years later.

This was done quietly and secretly while George was out of town. Incredibly enough, his mother lied to George and claimed that Frank had killed himself, and George believed her. This would be an ominous aspect of George's life for his later biographers—since at least according to the traditional narrative—George was said to have also ended his life by suicide.

At any rate, George grew up, graduated from high school, and went on to continue his studies in theatre at the local community college in Pasadena, California. George's first big break in Hollywood came when he was given a small part in 1939, classic film, "Gone with the Wind." After this gig ran its course, George pursued several bit parts in various theatrical productions, including a piece called "Pancho."

It was this role that saw him recruited by the Warner Brothers film company. It was upon getting signed with Warner Brothers that George adopted the name of "Reeves," which he would use for all future productions. He would play roles in several mediocre films over the next few years for Warner Brothers, but none of them gained much traction. World War II broke out in the meantime, and in 1943 Reeves put his acting career on hold when he was recruited by the U.S. Air Force.

Upon his return to civilian life, it was initially hard for George to get back into the swing of things in Hollywood. It was when he became involved with a woman named Toni Mannix however that all of that changed. Toni was actually the wife of MGM mogul, Eddie Mannix.

Toni liked George and helped him find work, she also struck up a romantic relationship with the budding star. It's been said that the relationship was an open secret, and Eddie approved of it. Eddie himself had several mistresses and apparently obliged his wife Toni to have some lovers on the side as well.

At any rate, it was through these new connections that George was eventually cast to play Superman for a TV pilot entitled "Superman and the Mole Men." It was this TV debut that led to Reeves starring in the eventual "Superman" TV series. The work was a major boon for Reeves at first, but after the first few years, he began to grow frustrated at what he saw as low pay and being typecast in one role.

Reeves began to feel he was at a dead-end, and would never be able to be famous for anything other than his performance as a TV Superman. Reeves eventually received a suitable pay increase, however, and things seemed to be looking up. In 1957, he was even optioned for a potential Superman film, "Superman and the Secret Planet."

The Reeves' world was rocked in 1958 in the meantime when he broke off relations with his biggest benefactor, Toni Mannix. He then became engaged to a woman named Leonore Lemmon. It's said that Toni Mannix was not too happy about these developments. The following year George Reeves would be dead.

The Disappearance

It was on June 16th, 1959 that George Reeves was found dead in his bedroom of what seemed to be a self-inflicted gunshot wound. He had several guests downstairs at his home, drinking and hanging out when the gunshot was allegedly heard. William Bliss allegedly ran up and found George lying on his bed, naked, with a gunshot wound to the head. The police were called shortly thereafter.

The Investigation

Although investigators seemed to view George Reeves'
death as an open and shut case of suicide, there are more
questions than answers. First of all, the abruptness of the
alleged suicide is very odd. It is true that George Reeves
was frustrated with his career, and feared being typecast as
Superman. But was this really enough of a reason for him
to suddenly resort to suicide?

He was trying to turn his career around after all. And
besides all of this, he had just begun a happy engagement
to the woman he loved. Would he throw all of that away in
one brief melancholy moment? Such a thing just didn't
seem to add up to those who knew George Reeves.

Another aspect that some later investigators have noted, is
that Toni Mannix was clearly enraged when George Reeves
ended their relationship. In her anger, she is said to have
had a kind of "I made you and I can break you" sort of
attitude about it. She was the one that made George
famous, and she felt betrayed that he would cut her off.

Her husband Eddie was a powerful guy and is said to have
had plenty of underworld connections with The Mob. It's
therefore been suggested that Eddie, angry that George
had upset his wife, had sent a mobster to take him out and
make it look like a suicide. This theory is admittedly a little
odd on the face of it. How often after all, does a guy have a
man killed because he *isn't having an affair with his wife?*

On the other hand, however, Toni and Eddie Mannix were
most definitely not your average couple. They had an open

marriage, yet held many secrets. And old Eddie Mannix was known as a Hollywood "fixer." Could it be that he fixed George for good, for making his wife cry?

The Suspects

Although the rest of the world put George Reeves' death out of their mind within mere weeks of its occurrence— among George's inner circle in Hollywood, there were always rumors of foul play. And most of them centered around Toni and Eddie Mannix. Interestingly enough, Reeves isn't the only Hollywood murder that Eddie Mannix himself has been accused of being involved in.

It's been suggested that when starlet Jean Harlow's screenwriter husband Paul Bern died of an apparent self-inflicted gunshot wound, it was actually a hit ordered by Eddie Mannix. So, we have two sketchy suicides in which Eddie Mannix was suspected of being involved. All of this, of course, is just unproven speculation. The gossip just wouldn't seem to die, however, and it was on Toni's deathbed in fact, that she supposedly made a last-minute confession of involvement.

In 1999 a Hollywood publicist by the name of Edward Lozzi claimed that he was at Toni's side when she passed and that he bore witness to her telling a priest that she had indeed sent a hitman to get George Reeves. According to Edward, he chose to come forward in 1999, because that was the year that the last of the "thugs" of Eddie Mannix had died, therefore clearing the way for disclosure. And the reason that Toni confessed to a priest before dying?

According to Lozzi, it was quite simple—he said that "she was absolutely terrified of going to hell."

But even if any of this is to be believed, there is still no explanation of who snuck into George's room that night to kill him. There has been some suggestion that William Bliss—the guy who had gone up to check on George on the night of his death—may have actually been the trigger man.

The whole crowd downstairs was very drunk, so it raises the possibility of all of them being duped into thinking that William went up to check on George after the gunshot when he really went up before the gun went off.

There is also the possibility that they were scared into concocting that story, lest they too fall victim to The Mob. Reeve's own fiancée Leonore Lemmon in fact, towards the end of her life, admitted that parts of her police testimony had been scripted and coached by Bliss. In the end, however, we will probably never really know the truth of what befell George Reeves that night.

In the End

Ruled a suicide, there was never any trial or conviction in this case.

The Strange Case of William Desmond Taylor

Who: William Desmond Taylor
Where: Los Angeles, California
When: 1922

Suspects: Edward Sands, Mabel Normand, Mary Miles Minter
Conviction: No conviction/Unsolved

Background Information

Hollywood pioneer William Desmond Taylor was born in Ireland on April 26th, 1872. William moved to the United States in 1891. Initially getting his start in New York, he married a woman and had a child. The traditional home life wasn't for Desmond, however, and he ran out on his family shortly thereafter, making his way to California in 1912. He then shifted gears and moved away from acting in favor of producing and directing instead.

The first film that he personally directed was 1914's "The Judge's Wife for Balboa." In 1915 he began work for "Famous Players-Lasky" (previously "Pallas Picture"). This company would become the main outlet for William's work. Besides a brief absence, while William served in World War I, he produced a steady stream of films with Famous Players.

In these films would appear some big-name actors of the time, such as Dustin Farnum and Mary Pickford. By 1920 he also had a successful trilogy on his hands based on Mark Twain's classic novel *Huckleberry Finn.* Also, around this time, he began directing a promising young starlet by the name of Mary Miles Minter, overseeing the production of the hit movie, "Anne of Green Gables".

It was while William Desmond Taylor was riding high in Hollywood that he was finally tracked down by the wife and child he had left behind in New York. His daughter Daisy, in fact, had begun writing to him. Taylor wrote back and agreed to meet up with his daughter on July 21st, 1921. The reunion was said to have been a pleasant one, and that they enjoyed each other's company. In less than a year's time, however, William Desmond Taylor would be murdered.

The Disappearance

William Desmond Taylor lost his life on February 2nd, 1922. His corpse was discovered at his personal residence in Los Angeles, California. Curious locals gathered when word got out that Mr. Taylor had passed. Seemingly out of nowhere, a man appeared on the scene claiming he was a physician. Curiously enough, this man looked William over and claimed that he died of a bleeding stomach. This assertion was ridiculous since it was soon found that William had been shot in the back. This mysterious "physician" was never seen again.

The Investigation

At the outset of William Desmond Taylor's murder, investigators had a difficult time establishing a motive. It didn't seem to be theft, since all of William's money and valuables were left undisturbed. Although there was plenty of clues on the scene, due to a lack of modern forensics and sloppiness on the part of investigators, no solid lead was ever established and the crime remained unsolved.

There was plenty of suspicious activity, however. For example, when investigators first arrived on the scene, it is said that they noticed a couple of big wig execs from Paramount tossing several pieces of paperwork into a burning fireplace. Also, there was one Mabel Normand a silent screen comedienne, who seemed to be "frantically looking for something."

The other odd thing about this case was the way that Desmond appeared to have been neatly put into position by the killer. He was laid flat on his back, his clothing straightened up, and his arms placed to his sides. With no sign of trauma, some thought he died of a medical issue. It wasn't until the corpse was flipped over that it was discovered that he had been shot.

As the investigation heated up, Taylor's home was thoroughly searched. From what was found, it was soon clear that William Desmond Taylor lived a double life— aside from the austere public image he cultivated as a professional director. Several nude photos were found of Desmond in compromised positions with various female actresses from his films. There was also the odd discovery of a "locked closet." Once open, the closet was found to be full of "women's lingerie."

The articles of clothing were apparently "tagged with initials and a date" indicating who they were from, and when William had acquired them during his sexual escapades. Along with lingerie, there was also a nightgown that belonged to one Mary Miles Minter, complete with her initials on the gown—*M. M. M.* Mary Miles Minter and William Desmond were close at the time of his death, and some would eventually suggest that she was close enough to be the killer.

They would also find a pink, perfume-drenched note from Mary Miles Minter, in which she proclaimed her undying love for Desmond. The missive read, "Dearest... I love you... I love you.... I love you.... Yours always! Mary!" Despite such an outpouring of love, the question remains— who hated this guy enough to kill him?

In the confusion of that day, the police did manage to speak with Mabel Normand and conducted a brief, on-the-spot interrogation as to what she was doing, and what her whereabouts were when William Desmond Taylor had passed. Mabel seemed to be honest with her remarks. She openly admitted that she had been ransacking the place in search of love letters that she herself had penned to Taylor, desperate to keep them from being circulated in the public sphere.

She seemed honest enough, but then again, for homicide detectives, everything should be suspect. Because as innocent as her remarks might have seemed, for all they knew, Mabel could have very well been searching for incriminating evidence that would link her to Desmond's death. In the initial phase of the investigation, the police did seem to pick up an important lead.

They spoke with one of William Desmond Taylor's neighbors, a lady named Faith Cole MacLean. Faith told detectives that she noticed something that startled her at the time of Desmond's death. Faith admittedly wasn't an expert on ballistics, but she knew that something dramatic had just happened at Demond's house. As she put it, "I wasn't sure then that it was a shot at all. But I distinctly heard an explosion." Not only that—she also may have seen the person behind the "explosion."

For Faith went on to report, "Then I glanced out of my window and I saw a man leaving the house and going down the walk." Before strangely adding, "I suppose it was a man!" Faith then went on to remark that the character she saw emerge from Desmond's home was rather hard to peg. She remarked about the figure, "It was dressed like a man, but, you know, funny looking. It was dressed in a heavy coat with a muffler around the chin and a cap pulled down over the eyes. But it walked like a woman—quick little steps and broad hips and short legs."

This was all well and good, but what really got the attention of investigators was Faith's claim that immediately before the "explosion" and the departure of the hulking figure, she had actually seen none other than Mabel Normand leaving the residence. But if this wasn't eyebrow-raising enough, according to nosy neighbor Faith, she had also seen Mary Miles Minter coming and going as well.

So, with this regular cast of characters milling about just prior to his death, there was more than enough suspicion to go around. Investigators followed up with Mabel shortly after this discovery, and once again she appeared to be honest and forthcoming. She confirmed that she had indeed been present at Desmond's house that night because he had invited her over to give her "a gift." The gift was apparently a new book by Sigmund Freud.

Desmond was a man of many interests, and he wanted to keep his peers enlightened as well. It was apparently his habit to supply reading materials to those close to him. Nothing all that unusual in that. But police would find evidence that Mabel and Desmond's relationship was far from just platonic. They would dig up love letters from Mabel which were stuffed—in all places—in Desmond's "riding boots." Were these the embarrassing notes that Mabel was trying to locate on the morning Desmond turned up dead?

Adding to the mystery, police would uncover a secret affair that Taylor was having with a woman named "Zelda Crosby" who was a screenwriter for Famous Players. They intended to contact her, but alarmingly enough, almost right after Desmond died, she was found dead of an apparent suicide. The mystery around this Hollywood mogul only seemed to grow by the minute, and so did the suspects.

The Suspects

As it pertains to solving the murder mystery of William Desmond Taylor, it wasn't that there weren't any suspects—it was that there were *way* too many potential suspects for the police to narrow it all down. Any one of his many lovers, or others attached to his lovers could have pulled the trigger. And the fact that the only eyewitness was never certain whether the hulking figure seen leaving the residence was a man or a woman, kept even the most basic details of a potential assailant, entirely obscure.

Along with all of these suspects, in the immediate days after William's demise, the police were actually swamped with several confessions. Unhinged individuals were calling the police station to claim involvement. Police knew that the calls they were getting were mostly just a bunch of cranks, but could one of them have been the actual killer?

Another suspect to emerge later on was Taylor's valet driver—Mr. Edward F. Sands. Edward parked cars for William, but he also did a little more than that. Because police came to find out, it was Sands who served as a photographer for Desmond's sexual escapades. Police learned that Taylor had fired Sands right before he was murdered.

This led police to the logical suspicion that perhaps Sands could have killed his former boss out of anger? The only trouble was, police had a heck of a time following this lead because shortly after Taylor's death, Mr. Sands disappeared. Try as they might, they couldn't find any trace of this guy ever again—which of course only made the situation seem all the more suspicious.

In the End

This case still remains unsolved, and one of the greatest real-life Hollywood murder mysteries of all time.

Kristi Johnson and Other Victims of A Hollywood Wannabe

Who*:* Kristi Johnson
Where: West Hollywood, California
When: February 2003
Suspect*:* Victor Palaeologus
Conviction*:* 2006

Background Information

Kristi Johnson was an aspiring model—or at least, that's what everyone told her she *should* be. Blessed with stunning looks and a perfect figure, she had been approached by random people for quite some time, people who complimented her, and even mentioned that perhaps she should give modeling a try. She never really took any of these people very seriously—she figured most were probably just desperate guys looking for a date.

But one fine day, she was out shopping when she bumped into a man who seemed to exude a sense of professionalism and purpose. And when he handed her a card and suggested she try out for modeling, she felt this guy's sales pitch was different from the rest. She felt that he really meant it.

And when he mentioned that he had a studio in a ritzy section of Hollywood she was sure that he wasn't just some low-life creep with a pick-up line. She thought he was legitimate. So, when this guy suggested she could meet up with him at 10:30 am on a Sunday, she decided that she would take him up on the offer.

The last soul to see Kristi alive was an elderly couple who lived in the neighborhood of the house Kristi was visiting for her supposed photo shoot. Kristi was having trouble finding the place and had asked the elderly man, who had been roaming about his front yard, for directions.

He initially had trouble giving them. He was startled by the sudden intrusion, and couldn't collect his thoughts well enough to be of much help. But the startled man's wife stepped forward and promptly explained that the house Kristi was looking for, was at the end of the street. That was the last that the world of the living would see of Kristi Johnson.

The Disappearance

It would later be discovered that Kristi Johnson met up with a supposed Hollywood agent/photographer who went by the name of Victor Thomas, on February 15th, 2003. Her worried family and friends notified the police that she had not come home shortly thereafter. She was living with a couple of roommates at the time, and one roommate in particular—Carrie Barrish, proved to be particularly helpful for investigators.

Upon being questioned, Carrie recalled that Kristi had mentioned that she had come across a man who claimed to be in the "filmmaking business." She was told that she would be auditioning for a part in a new James Bond picture. This piece of information was important because it would later match the description given by Susan Murphy—a would-be victim—who managed to slip out of the maniac's grasp.

Similar to Susan's account, Kristi had also told Carrie that she might be able to make up to $100,000 for the gig. Carrie told investigators that Kristi had bought some very specific articles of clothing for the supposed audition: "a white long-sleeved shirt made of very nice, soft cotton with a pointed collar, a black miniskirt, black pumps with six-inch stiletto heels, and a pair of sheer pantyhose."

These clothes matched up with the same kind of dress that the one who got away—Susan Murphy—was told to wear. It was also helpful to detectives that Carrie Barrish recalled that Kristi was supposed to meet the Hollywood photographer at a house in Beverly Hills. Police actually issued a public statement a few days after Kristi's disappearance, on Wednesday, February 17th, 2003.

The statement read in part, "On February 17th, 2003, the Santa Monica Police Department began a missing person investigation regarding the disappearance of Kristine Louise Johnson. The preliminary investigation disclosed that Ms. Johnson was last seen leaving her residence in Santa Monica on the afternoon of February 15th."

The public statement then went on to say, "Family and friends have not heard from her since Saturday and are concerned about her safety. She may have been en route to an appointment with a possible photographer in the area of Beverly Hills. Ms. Johnson was last seen driving her 1996 Mazda Miata convertible. Anyone with information is encouraged to call the Office of Criminal Investigations tip line."

The Investigation

Once she was reported missing, the investigation into her disappearance began. Initially, police hit a bunch of dead ends and false leads. They looked into several people including Kristi's former boyfriend, but all of the usual suspects had rock-solid alibis. Investigators obviously had no idea that Kristi had made the fateful decision to hook up with a stranger. It would soon be discovered, however, and, tipped off by Kristi's friends as to what she was up to, detectives would try to get the word out.

Efforts included an article featured in the "Los Angeles Times" which solemnly proclaimed, "A 21-year-old Santa Monica woman who may have been on her way to Beverly Hills to meet a photographer, has not been seen for five days, police said Wednesday." The article then went on to state that unspecified "friends" had tipped the police off "that Johnson was supposed to meet a photographer, possibly to pose for pictures, on Saturday. Anyone with information about Johnson's whereabouts is asked to call the police."

Police would then receive another tip when a woman named Susan Murphy notified them that she too had been propositioned by a Beverly Hills photographer recently. She had read the article and was alarmed at how similar the details sounded to recent events in her own life. She too had been approached by a random man, propositioning her to model for him, and promising a big payout if she would come down to his place in Beverly Hills to audition.

She explained how the man had approached her in a very professional manner, stating that he could get her a gig to be a "James Bond girl." This was in the early 2000s after all, when James Bond was just then returning to the big screen. Images of her being the next Hollywood vixen immediately flashed before her eyes. For a young woman like Susan, it sounded like she was being given the chance of a lifetime.

Susan still wasn't sure if her experience was connected to what she read about the missing woman—Kristi Johnson—but she called the police tip line anyway. And detectives were certainly glad that she did. Because for them, her account seemed like the most promising lead they had. For if Susan truly had encountered the same man, they not only had a lead but a direct eyewitness to their person of interest and soon to be suspect.

And fortunately for them, Susan proved to be an excellent eyewitness at that. She described the man as being in his mid to late thirties. She described his blue eyes, and his curly dark brown, slightly thinning hair, which framed his circular face. She also recalled that he was beardless, and sported a baseball cap. She recalled how he wore a pair of khakis and a stylish brown jacket.

She claimed that the man approached her saying that he was in the employ of a company called "Silver Screen Partners" which was supposed "an affiliate of Walt Disney" and indicated that he thought she would be good screen material. Susan recalled the guy saying his name was Victor Thomas. Detectives were thankful to get such a promising lead and ready to follow it wherever it took them.

Prior to Kristi's disappearance, Susan herself had ended up having coffee with the guy who continued to insist that she would be a shoo-in for a new James Bond movie. He even promised that once she was recruited, she would bag an easy $100,000 dollars for the role. Susan was interested, but something in the back of her mind made her hesitate. She was soon overwhelmed with the prospect of a Hollywood celebrity, however, when Victor promised that when she showed up at the studio, he would be able to personally introduce her to both Sean Connery and Pierce Brosnan.

Feeling like she couldn't let such a chance slip through her fingers, Susan finally agreed to audition. That's when Victor became quite specific. He instructed her that she needed to wear a "black miniskirt" which was "as short and tight as possible" along with "a white button-up shirt." He also insisted she wears stockings, high heels, and wears her hair in a ponytail. Fortunately for Susan Murphy, she happened to have a very keen and alert fiancé.

After her meeting with Victor Thomas, she came home and informed her fiancé, Mark Wilson of what had transpired. Alarm bells immediately went off in Mark's mind. Susan agreed that some aspects of the encounter seemed a little sketchy but she still wanted to check back with Victor just in case she really could land the role of a lifetime. Mark most definitely didn't want her to go, but the two managed to work out a compromise. She would show up, but he would take her and park his car a short distance from the meet-up site so that he could keep an eye on the situation the whole time.

This would prove to be pivotal. As planned, Mark dropped Susan off at the site and parked a short distance down the street from the house where the audition was supposed to be. Susan, not wanting to stand around outside in a short miniskirt, ended up defying Vitor's instructions of being dressed and ready for the rehearsal by wearing cargo pants instead. She had the skirt in a plastic bag with her and figured she would change into it later if the whole thing turned out to be legitimate.

She stood outside the house wondering when Victor's car might pull up, when suddenly she heard his voice right in her ear saying, "That isn't what I told you to wear! I'm going to take you somewhere to change." She was startled that the guy seemed to just pop up at her like that. Obviously, he had walked over, and she didn't even see him approach. Victor must have seen her startled reaction, prompting Victor to change his approach as he suggested, "Let's go somewhere to have a drink and talk about the role. It will help you get very prepared."

Victor then put his hand on Susan's shoulder as if to steer her toward the direction he wanted her to walk. Susan not enjoying the feeling of being pushed around, objected, "I'm not going anywhere with you until I see some identification." This prompted Victor to scowl and make up a lame excuse about having left his ID behind. As Susan tried to pull away, Victor then turned up the heat by challenging her, "You're giving up the opportunity of a lifetime." Susan wasn't having it however as she shot back, "You know—actually—my safety is much more important!"

This only seemed to make Victor more determined, however, as he offered, "We need to go. We should go and meet my friend Natasha and talk about the role." Susan had never heard this guy mention anything about any "Natasha" before, and to her, it seemed that he was just making stuff up as he went along. Growing ever more fearful, Susan took a few steps back from the raving maniac, prompting him to shout, "Okay, just forget it! I don't think you are right for the part anyway. Forget it!"

Susan's fiancé Mark in the meantime, seeing the aggressive behavior, couldn't help but intervene. He pulled his car forward a few feet, parked, and quickly hopped out of the vehicle. He then sprinted right up to Victor to confront him. Susan ran toward her man, just as Victor suddenly bolted in the other direction. Mark and Susan then rushed off to the car and began chasing after Victor as he ran on foot.

If any bystanders saw this crazy pursuit, of a couple driving around town, chasing after a thin, balding middle-aged man running on foot—it must have looked pretty bizarre.

Nevertheless, Mark was determined to catch this guy. And as Victor ran down alleys and behind buildings, Mark finally managed to corner him. He then hopped out of the car and confronted him directly.

It's important to note that Mark used to be a cop, and although he was no longer on the force at the time of this encounter, he pretty much behaved as if he was. After getting ahold of the man, he patted him down for weapons. It was once he was confident that the now cowering Victor didn't have a gun on his person, that Mark shouted, "I don't know if I'm going to kill you or drag you to the police station."

Mark then grilled the man about who he was and who he worked for. Victor then blathered some story about working for Disney. Yet, even though Victor still pretended to at least in some fashion, be in the employ of the Hollywood film industry, he seemed to acknowledge that he was up to no good. Because Victor whimpered to Mark that he would "never do it again."

Mark then demanded Victor's phone number, and the guy rattled off one for him. Mark wanted to verify it, so he went to his car to get his cellphone. It was while his back was turned that Victor once again took off and ran right into a busy intersection, almost getting run over by oncoming traffic. Mark later tried to call the number that the guy gave, but it proved to be phony.

Susan initially thought about filing a police report, but after considering that no actual crime had been committed, she wasn't sure what she would report the guy for, so she decided to just let it go. It was when she heard Kristi Johnson's story however that she knew she had to come forward.

Susan Murphy's account was indeed important and would have police scouring security camera footage from the Century City Mall to see if any clues could be picked up. In the meantime, Susan provided her description of the guy to a sketch artist who was able to render a composite sketch of the shadowy creep who called himself Victor Thomas. Susan was then a big help once again when she confirmed that a freeze-frame from the mall's security camera had captured the baseball cap-wearing Victor Thomas on tape. The brief, grainy footage of Victor was not very detailed, but it was a start.

As the days wore on in the meantime, teams of investigators scoured locales such as Topanga Canyon, San Fernando Valley, and the Santa Monica Mountains, just in case a killer might have discarded his prey. These areas were indeed known by police as popular dumping grounds for murderers.

The next major break in the case arrived when it was discovered that Susan's Mazda had been parked at a local hotel by a guy matching Victor's description. The guy had come in early in the morning and attempted to park the vehicle himself. A valet, parking attendant had stopped him and advised that the spot was for "valet parking only." The guy then simply tossed the attendant the keys and remarked, "Well—valet it then."

The parking attendant was shown the composite sketch of Victor and he confirmed that this was indeed the man that he saw that day. With this confirmation, the police brought in a K-9 unit to see if the dogs could pick up Kristi Johnson's scent. After several tries with K-9s however, the dogs were unable to render any results. As it turns out investigators wouldn't need K-9s—soon they would have a lead that would lead them right to the suspect.

The Suspect

Shortly after the composite sketch of "Victor Thomas" made the rounds, police were alerted by a parole officer by the name of Maryanne Larios that she believed she had dealings with the suspect. She informed them that the guy from the sketch was actually named Victor Palaeologus and that he had been out on parole from prison. Just released in fact, a little over a month prior, after doing time for grand theft auto.

The short time frame made police skeptical, but when Maryanne mentioned that the former parolee had been known to impersonate a Hollywood mogul, and had even conned women into thinking he could get them a gig on a James Bond film—the lead was just too on target to pass up.

As it turns out, it wasn't very hard to find this Victor character, since the parolee was already back in jail on new charges of grand theft auto (he was a serial car thief), unrelated to Kristi's disappearance. A brief look at Victor Palaeologus' rap sheet also verified that he had used the

Hollywood schtick in the past since he was arrested for attempted rape in 1989 after luring a young woman to his hotel room with similar claims of turning her into a star.

Rather than auditioning, however, Victor savagely assaulted her, ripping at her clothes and attempting to tie her up. Fortunately for this victim, she was able to break free of his grip, and her screams in the hotel hallway brought forth the protection of a fellow patron as well as a hotel security guard. Victor tried to run from the scene but was arrested a short time later.

But now that Victor was once again back behind bars, investigators had to figure out what to do next. At this point, it wasn't even known if Kristi was still alive—all they knew was that they had the man in custody who most likely caused her to vanish. Could they link him to this still-unfolding crime with charges that would stick?

In order to further establish Victor as a suspect, police had their main eyewitness, Susan Murphy come in and identify Victor in a lineup. With Victor lined up with other criminals, Susan was immediately able to pick him out of the crowd. Police then attempted to interrogate Victor about what he knew of Kristi Johnson, but Palaeologus refused to talk.

At one point he seemed to slightly slip up when he mentioned hearing the "news reports" and "knowing what detectives were after." After this, the detective who was questioning him demanded to know, "What do you think I'm after?" Realizing he might be about to incriminate himself, Victor then clammed up entirely and demanded to have an attorney present.

It was shortly after this exchange that Kristi Johnson's body was found buried in a remote stretch of hills in West Hollywood. Her decomposing body was zipped up in a sleeping bag, and her hands were tied behind her back. The missing person's case was now a homicide case, and the suspected killer—Victor Palaeologus—was about to stand trial.

In the End

The trial of Victor Palaeologus first convened in the summer of 2006. The prosecution was working with limited information as to what actually transpired to Kristi once she met Victor. The working theory was that Victor had attempted to rape Kristi after luring her to a secluded area, as had been his penchant in the past.

It was theorized that Victor began strangling Kristi when she resisted his advances. It was then suggested that perhaps Victor didn't even mean to kill her, but once he did—he decided to dump her body. One thing was clear, the sleeping bag that he had placed Kristi in, was actually taken from Kristi's own car. The fact that he used her own sleeping bag to dispose of Kristi's remains, would seem to indicate a much more spontaneous event than anything planned.

An autopsy also seemed to suggest that strangulation wasn't what killed Kristi but rather blunt force trauma to the head, which she appeared to have sustained after Victor tossed her from the car. It was theorized that she might have still been alive but unconscious prior to being thrown from the vehicle. It was only when her head slammed into a rock as her comatose body, zipped up in a sleeping bag, rolled down that Hollywood hill, that her life came to an end.

In the face of the charges against him, Victor was initially defiant as usual, and his defense team fought to prove his supposed innocence. The defense team must not have been doing a very good job, however, because just a few weeks into the trial, Victor did an about-face and decided it would be in his best interest to cop a plea deal and confess to the killing.

As part of his plea deal, Victor was given 25 to life, rather than the death sentence that he otherwise would have received. But this wasn't the end of the story, however, because a short time later, Victor decided to make a motion to withdraw his previous confession. He had decided to plead not guilty after all.

The judge wasn't going to have it, however, and in the courtroom, he flatly remarked, "I'm going to deny the motion, Mr. Palaeologus. The law states clearly that a plea cannot be withdrawn simply because the defendant has changed his mind." And as such, the judge declared that the previous sentence that would have Palaeologus serving 25 years to life, would stand.

Hollywood vs. Vaughn Greenwood

Who*:* Multiple
Where: Hollywood, California
When: 1960s and 1970s
Suspects*:* Vaughn Greenwood
Conviction*:* 1976

Background Information

Police detectives have a tough job, and more often than not their finely honed hunches pay off. But there are times when their assumptions are indeed wrong, and they end up going down the wrong track. And sometimes it's only after going around in circles and ending up on a wild goose chase that they realize a mistake has been made. This is precisely what happened during the investigation into serial murderer Vaughn Greenwood.

From 1964 to 1975 Greenwood rocked California with multiple killings. The killings had all the hallmarks of a serial killer, complete with a repetitive profile of victims—primarily middle-aged hobos—as well as a signature method of killing by way of a butcher knife. It was this gruesome calling card that led to the perpetrator being nicknamed the "Slasher."

The Disappearance

The victims of Vaughn Greenwood are numerous—with eleven known souls being slaughtered by this killer. The first was David Russel, who turned up dead in 1964. And the last to die was a guy named Clyde Hays, in January of 1975. His final victim was a man named William Graham, who actually managed to survive the ordeal. The murders were truly hideous affairs, in which Greenwood had slashed his victims' throats, and in some cases, even tried to lap up their blood.

The Investigation

Even though the killer's prolific killings were uniform and several clues were left behind, investigators seemed perplexed when it came to finding leads for this case. And it wasn't until January 31st, 1975 that they worked up a profile complete with a composite rendering of the perpetrator. Police then announced that they had their man. They proclaimed that he was "a Caucasian male in his late 20s or early 30s, six feet tall and 190 pounds, with shoulder-length blond hair, and some visible deformity."

With such descriptive details, one might think that detectives must be right on the verge of bagging this creep. And the descriptors went much deeper than that, because they also described him as being "a sexually impotent coward, venting his own feelings of worthlessness on hapless derelicts and down and outers."

Suddenly the police detectives seemed to know this dude on a personal level, with such detailed psychoanalysis at their disposal. For all of their confidence and bluster, shortly thereafter, much of this data would be proved entirely wrong. Despite the fact that the police declared that the perpetrator was a blond-haired Caucasian for example— Vaughn Greenwood was an African American.

And even though the police for some reason insisted that the killer had some sort of obvious deformity, as if he were some hideous, hunchbacked Quasimodo lurking in the night—Vaughn was perfectly healthy and in great shape. But despite their failure to physically identify the killer, it seems that the detectives' remarks about Vaughn being a loner and a misfit did indeed strike a nerve with this sociopath.

The actual killer, Vaughn himself it turns out, was upset that the profilers got it wrong—so much so that he was apparently driven to solve the case for them. It was after a brutal slaying at a residence in Hollywood on February 2nd, 1975 that the Slasher left the police a little note—*with his own personal address on it!*

The killer actually dropped the note off in the adjoining driveway near the home of his murder victim. That driveway belonged to none other than Hollywood legend Burt Reynolds. It was after Burt personally handed the note off to police that Vaughn, who had eluded authorities for a whole decade, was quite easily tracked down and caught.

The Suspects

As mentioned, police were on the wrong trail, looking for a killer who didn't exist. It took the actions of Vaughn Greenwood himself to alert authorities to the true suspect of these crimes. It could be speculated that Greenwood himself wished to be caught. Such an idea is not unheard of, since some compulsive killers ultimately long for their own arrest so that their sick compulsions will come to an end.

In the End

Vaughn then stood trial in 1976 and was found guilty as charged for the 11 killings that he'd been linked to at the time. And on January 19th, 1977 he was sentenced to spend the rest of his natural life behind bars. He was given a life sentence. Interestingly enough, he was put on a second trial for the terrible attack on two people who survived his onslaught—for this, he had 32 years tacked onto his sentence.

Bruce Lee
Who Silenced this Martial Artist?

Who: Bruce Lee
Where: Hong Kong, China

When: July 1973
Suspects: Betty Ting Pei/Enemies from Various Martial
Arts Circles
Conviction: No Conviction/Unsolved

Background Information

Bruce Lee, the martial arts legend, was born in San
Francisco, California, but grew up in Hong Kong in the
1950s. This was Hong Kong prior to its takeover by
communist China, when it was still a dominion of the British
Empire. The Hong Kong of Bruce Lee's youth was a
thriving, capitalist democracy comparable to Taiwan, South
Korea, and Japan.

Hong Kong was the perfect cauldron that mixed ancient
Chinese culture with modern, liberal concepts such as
theatre and the arts. Bruce Lee was a student of the
ancient Chinese martial arts practice of kung fu from a
young age, and after finishing his primary education, began
to get involved in the budding film industry in Hong Kong.
Bruce Lee had a penchant for getting into street fights,
however, and after a bad run-in with the police, his father
agreed to send him back to America, to stay with his aunt in
California.

Bruce then went to high school, moved around a bit, and
tried some college, before getting involved in martial arts
contests in California. He also began to instruct others. It
was when he began to instruct others on how to perform
Chinese-based martial arts that other Chinese martial
artists began to warn Lee not to teach "outsiders" the fine

art. There were those in the community you see, who apparently did not wish for martial arts skills to be handed on to those who did not hail from East Asia.

Lee ignored the warnings, however, and continued refining his skills and training others. He also began doing a bit of dabbling into acting. It was this work that would lead him on a path directly to Hollywood. Lee was cast in a regular TV series, called "The Green Hornet."

The show aired for just one brief season, from the Fall of 1966 to the Spring of 1967, but it managed to get its toes wet in the world of production. He then attempted to launch his big break in Hollywood but was actually advised to make it big in Hong Kong first. So it was that Lee went back to his old stomping grounds of Hong Kong where he already had a large fan base for his work on "The Green Hornet."

Once back in Hong Kong, he starred in his first feature-length film, "The Big Boss" which premiered in 1971. The film was a hit, and was quickly followed by "Fist of Fury" and then the legendary "Way of the Dragon" both completed in 1972. These successes were then followed by the blockbuster "Enter the Dragon" which was finished up in the Spring of 1973.

The film would go on to become a massive success, but Lee wouldn't have long to relish what he had done, since his life would come to an end before the movie was even released.

On that Day

Bruce Lee, at the age of 32, appeared to have the beginnings of an unknown yet serious health condition. And on May 10th, 1973 he demonstrated as much when he suddenly fell to the floor while working on some extra dialogue for "Enter the Dragon" in Hong Kong. He appeared to even go into seizures.

Placed in an ambulance he was taken to Hong Kong Baptist Hospital. Here he was found to have been suffering from swelling of the brain and was prescribed mannitol to decrease the swelling. Lee was fine for a time, but then on July 20th, 1973 he and producer Raymond Chow went to the apartment of a Taiwanese actress by the name of Betty Ting Pei.

Shortly thereafter, Raymond Chow left Bruce Lee and Betty Ting Pei alone, to attend to other business. According to Betty Ting Pei's later testimony, she gave Lee a painkiller called Equagesic which is said to be a mixture of meprobamate and aspirin. Upon Chow's return, he found Lee unconscious, in Betty's bed.

After being unable to rouse Lee out of his stupor, an ambulance was summoned, and he was sent to Queen Elizabeth Hospital. At this point, Lee was already dead and the final pronouncement of his death was confirmed at the hospital.

The Investigation

Lee's death was indeed mysterious, but there wasn't much of an investigation, since it was assumed that he had suffered from some sort of medical health episode. But really the only person who knows exactly what Lee's final moments were like, was the Taiwanese actress whom he was staying with—Betty Ting Pei. And strangely enough, she made herself appear very suspicious after Lee's death.

Rather than giving a full account of what happened, Betty Ting Pei initially denied that she was even present. And after reporters began to pump her for information on the night in question, she claimed she wasn't there. She went on the record to state, "On Friday night when he died, I was not at home—I had gone out with my mother."

This was obviously not true, yet for some reason, Betty Ting Pei fed this bald-faced lie to reporters. Those that know the actress are certain that she did this in her panicked state, out of not wanting to be associated with Lee's passing, and perhaps even in an effort to distance herself from a perceived affair. Yet all she managed to do by lying, was make herself look incredibly suspicious. And it was in the vacuum of knowledge that people began to talk.

Wild gossip was regularly printed in tabloid newspapers in Hong Kong. And things got so bad for Betty Ting Pei, she virtually went into hiding. Some fans were so upset at the idea that perhaps she had something to do with Bruce Lee's death, they even tried their hand at becoming vigilante investigators.

The threat of one of these crazed fans doing something terrible became so bad, that Hong Kong authorities eventually got involved in the matter. In order to satiate the public, they finally realized that they had no choice but to conduct a thorough investigation into the circumstances surrounding Bruce Lee's death.

The Suspect

Although many shadowy groups and people have been cited in multiple conspiracy theories, the only tangible suspect in Lee's death is Betty Ting Pei. Pei for her part—at least when she wasn't fabricating the details of the event—has always proclaimed her innocence. She has also been quick to point out how her life had been irrevocably affected by the aftermath of Lee's death.

She later did openly admit to giving Bruce a pain killer, and medical experts concurred that Bruce who was already on medication for a previous back injury, most likely had a bad reaction to the medication. As for Betty Ting Pei, her film career had sputtered to a halt by the end of the 1970s, and by the early 1980's she had retired altogether from show business, living a quiet and secluded life thereafter.

It seems that after Ms. Pei, the most visible suspect, went into seclusion, that the more elaborate conspiracy theories as to the cause of Bruce Lee's death began to circulate. The most infamous of which was the "delayed death strike" theory. It was well known that Bruce Lee had enemies in the traditional martial arts world. And it has been surmised that some of these traditionalists, irked by the fact that

Bruce had taken the sacred knowledge of the trade to the mainstream, wanted to have him killed.

One theory was that a martial arts expert might have paid Bruce a visit in Hong Kong where he/she administered the "delayed death strike" to silence Bruce Lee's spilling of ancient secrets, once and for all. And just what is the *delayed death strike?* Supposedly this rare ability is only known by a few supreme martial arts experts, in which they can focus their internal energy, then touch their intended victim on a specific pressure point, and release a powerful vibratory pulse, which will affect the afflicted person's circulatory system.

Could this be why Bruce suddenly became so ill on that day in May, in 1973? Was this just the first instance of the delayed death strike at work? And then he finally succumbed to its effects that July? It all sounds pretty far-fetched, but this conspiracy theory remains widely circulated to this very day. A perhaps, slightly more believable conspiracy theory has also made the rounds— which while easier to believe—contains the same exact motive of the previous one.

It's been suggested that perhaps Lee at some point, had been slipped a special Chinese herbal concoction, which sickened him and eventually caused his death. The shadowy suspects of this alleged hit, are also the same supposed martial arts masters, who supposedly killed Lee for the same reason as previously mentioned—because he was spilling too many secrets about the art.

Karate expert Ben Block for one has championed this theory. Mr. Block has pointed out that traditional Chinese herbal concoctions could possibly evade a typical autopsy, rendering the true cause of Bruce Lee's death completely unknown.

In the End

Bruce Lee's death still remains a mystery and continues to be open to speculation.

Gary Devore
The Hollywood Screenwriter
Who Knew Too Much?

Who*:* Gary Devore
Where: Santa Barbara, California
When: July 1997
Suspects*:* Unknown
Conviction*:* No conviction/Case unsolved

Background Information

Gary Devore was born on September 17th, 1941. He grew up to be a gifted writer, and in the 1960s Mr. Devore began working as a professional screenwriter for television productions such as "The Newlywed Game" and "The Steve Allen Show." Devore was also famous for marrying vocalist Maria Cole. Ms. Cole, of course, was the daughter of singing legend—Nat King Cole.

The couple parted ways in 1978 however, and Gary would go on to marry three more women. He married Sandie Newton, before their split in 1985, and then Claudia Christian whom he divorced in 1992, and then his last and final wife Wendy Devore, with whom he remained married until his tragic death in 1997.

Gary Devore was a favorite in Hollywood circles and friends with the likes of Arnold Schwarzenegger, who starred in the film "Raw Deal", a film based on Gary's screenplay. Gary was appreciated for both his believable dialogue and his ability to weave complex and intriguing plots. Little did he know that his own life would turn into something akin to a Hollywood thriller.

Disappearance

Gary Devore went missing in June of 1997 after driving back from Santa Fe, New Mexico, to Santa Barbara, California. No one—at least among his own inner circle—quite knew what had happened to him at the time. It was nearly a full year later that Gary Devore's Ford Explorer was found with his dead body inside. The vehicle was discovered in Palmdale, California, inside an aqueduct, lodged underneath a bridge.

The Investigation

Right before screenwriter Gary Devore's disappearance, he was having trouble finishing up his latest script. He was being plagued with a little something some writers occasionally refer to as "writer's block." He actually left California for Santa Fe, New Mexico, in order to clear his mind, and help him come up with some new ideas. He was scheduled to come back that day, but after his spouse, Wendy had not heard from him for several hours after the appointed time slated for his return—she called him around 1 in the morning.

She finally did manage to get a hold of her husband, but he seemed to be rushed and there was a lack of general details as it pertained to his whereabouts. It was a year later that investigators would finally find Gary Devore—but figuring out exactly what happened to him and who might be responsible was a whole other story. The circumstances surrounding the discovery of Gary's corpse were very strange.

His laptop which is said to have had his latest screenplay "The Big Steal" saved on its hard drive, had apparently *been stolen.* Even more distressing, this writer whose fingers had pummeled countless keyboards, crafting incredible tales, had his hands cut clean off. Since his hands wouldn't be chopped off from simply a car accident, it was quite obvious that he was the victim of foul play.

The surrounding area of the aqueduct, under the bridge, also showed no sign of an accident. It was more like the car was just slowly rolled down into it. But after all of these initial findings came to light, a more sinister, potential motive for Gary's killing would begin to emerge.

The Suspects

According to those closest to Gary Devore, his latest script "The Big Steal" was nothing short of an indictment of the U.S. invasion of Panama in the 1980s. For some, they couldn't help but wonder if perhaps someone in the CIA didn't like what Gary was revealing, and decided to silence him. Devore allegedly discovered that the real reason for the invasion of Panama was to retrieve evidence of American diplomats in compromised conditions.

Yes, as far fetched as it may sound, it was suggested that the Panamanian dictator Manuel Noriega, had been entertaining high-level officials from the White House at his own residence and that he had secretly filmed diplomats having sexual relations with women at his many drunken revelries.

Noriega was supposedly getting ready to use these sex tapes to blackmail the U.S. The premise of Gary's screenplay, therefore, was that the whole war on Panama was simply an effort on the part of the U.S. to steal the compromising data back—hence "The Big Steal."

Whatever the case may be, it seems that someone was very interested in this new screenplay of Gary's, because the laptop on which the final draft of it was saved, has never been returned. Adding to the mystery, Gary Devore's widow Wendy has confirmed that he was actually in talks with the CIA, and allegedly received regular calls from government agents.

Even more intriguing, an official who worked for the George H. W. Bush administration has suggested that Gary Devore was well known by the CIA and had gone with CIA operatives to Panama in the past.

In the End

No trial, conviction, or suspect has ever been arrested in this strange and mysterious case.

Natalie Wood—Musings of Murder and Mystery Over Dark Waters

Who: Natalie Wood
Where: Hollywood, California
When: November 1981
Suspects: H
Conviction: No conviction/Unsolved

Background Information

Many are not aware of this fact, but the actress the world has come to know as Natalie Wood began life as Natalia Nikolaevna Zakharenko. She had long ago picked the name "Natalie Wood" as her Hollywood-friendly name, shedding her birth appellation, which was indicative of her Russian ancestry.

Although today Hollywood is much more diverse and welcoming of people of all backgrounds, the Hollywood of several decades ago was a much less accepting environment. Actors often changed their names to make them more "friendly" to American audiences. The creation of the "Natalie Wood" persona was a result of these pressures at work.

Her parents were indeed Russian immigrants. Having fled the aftermath of the communist takeover of Russia, her parents would long regale her with tales of Russia's pre-communist days, often speaking at length of their admiration of the last Russian royal family, the Romanovs. Natalie's mother Maria would later claim that they were related to the Romanovs, whom the Russian communists had slaughtered.

Most dismiss any such notion as nothing more than her often imaginative mother's fanciful musings. One musing that would later come back to haunt the Natalie Wood case, was the fact that Maria supposedly went to a gypsy fortune-teller before Natalie was born and was told that she should stay away from "dark water." According to this gypsy mystic, there was a chance that she could meet her death through it.

Because of this prediction, Maria would be convinced of the possibility that she might drown, and for the rest of her life avoided water as much as possible. With such a fear of water in mind, one can only imagine how petrified Maria must have been when she crossed over the oceans to get to America!

Nevertheless, she arrived on American shores without a scratch. Little did she know that while she would safely avoid a water-logged fate, it would be her daughter Natalie Wood who would later be found dead in the water. Maria had no way of knowing that the gypsy's grim forecast would skip a generation.

Natalie Wood's Hollywood career began at a young age. She was only eight years old when she was cast in a leading role for the Christmas holiday classic "Miracle on 34th Street" which made its debut in 1947. Both the movie and Natalie herself were a hit. Wood would then go on to appear in several more films throughout her childhood and young adult years.

She ended up marrying fellow famed actor Robert Wagner in 1957 but divorced him in 1962. Several failed relationships would follow before she married film producer Robert Gregson in 1969. It was with Gregson that Wood had her first child, named "Natasha" in her honor.

Natalie and Robert Gregson's marriage was dissolved however in 1972. Later that year Wood actually remarried her former husband Robert Wagner, with whom she would have her next child—Courtney—who was born in 1974. It was about ten years later, that Wood would somehow fall off the back of a boat near California's Santa Catalina Island, and slip from this world for good.

On that Day

It was on November 28th, 1981 that Natalie Wood, along with her husband Robert Wagner, fellow actor Christopher Walken, and the ship's captain—Dennis Davern—all set sail for the open waters between the coast of Southern California and Santa Catalina Island.

At some point, Natalie left the boat and ended up in the water. Her dead body would be found six hours later. The question that investigators have been asking ever since, is whether she slipped and fell, or was thrown overboard—or perhaps even jumped of her own volition, in an effort to commit suicide. The questions surrounding her death would be numerous. The answers, however, would be few and far between.

The Investigation

The investigation into Natalie Wood's death began shortly after Natalie was found to be missing. Interestingly enough, Natalie's own husband wanted to call off the search after just a couple of hours. His apparent lack of enthusiasm has fueled speculation that perhaps he had something to do with his wife's death. Nevertheless, the search continued and after 6 hours, they did indeed find the drowned, lifeless body of Natalie Wood.

After the recovery of her corpse, the fact that she had several bruises on her arms and legs and a laceration to her cheek, sparked suspicion. After an autopsy, however, it was determined that the injuries were most likely sustained from an accidental fall from the boat and the subsequent struggle of trying to get back on board. These findings were called into question, however, and the argument has remained that perhaps the injuries were more consistent with someone being tossed overboard, than with someone simply accidentally falling off the deck of a ship.

Adding to this speculation was the fact that the captain of the ship—Davern—came forward in 2011 to confirm that Robert Wagner and Natalie Wood were in a heated argument on the night she drowned. Even more chilling, Davern claims that the last thing he heard Robert Wagner say to Natalie Wood at the end of their argumentative exchange was, "Get off my f***** boat!"

Making the matter even more incriminating was what Captain Davern described as some rather peculiar actions on the part of Robert Wagner after they realized that Natalie

Wood was missing. Davern claims that Robert Wagner actually insisted that he not use any searchlights to find Natalie.

This left his wife Natalie alone, submerged and unaccounted for in the completely "dark waters" that had been foretold by that Russian gypsy so long ago. As chilling as it all sounds, Robert Wagner seemed intent to allow the long foretold family prophecy to finally come to fruition.

The Suspects

Robert Wagner's actions on the night of Natalie Wood's demise, do indeed strike one as rather strange and suspicious. But just to play the devil's advocate for Robert Wagner, a man who has always professed his innocence, perhaps he had a valid reason not to use searchlights that night. It's hard for us to second guess and understand his reasoning, but maybe he was considering something that most observers are not.

Wagner, Walken, and Woods were all three, big Hollywood stars after all, and Wagner perhaps just didn't want to call attention to themselves. It was perhaps a selfish, neurotic, and misguided thing for Wagner to do, but it doesn't necessarily mean that he was trying to cover up the murder of his wife.

Ship captain, Dennis Davern does paint a dark picture of that night, however, suggesting that Robert Wagner was upset with his wife for "flirting" with their guest Christopher Walken. Woods and Walken were currently working on a film called "Brainstorm," together and apparently had become quite close. Was it this closeness that sent Robert Wagner into a jealous enough rage to kill his wife?

Although Christopher Walken for his part has remained fairly silent about the whole incident, Davern claims that Wagner and Walken even got into a shouting match at one point. Davern would later recall hearing Wagner shout at Walken, "What are you trying to do? F*** my wife?"

According to Dennis Davern, it was after this, that a disgusted Natalie Woods ran off to her room on the yacht, and Wagner followed her. According to Davern when he next saw Wagner he was agitated and alone, "sweating profusely" in fact, in a clear indication that something was terribly wrong. Davern tried to ignore the alarm bells going off in his mind, however, and it wasn't until around 1:30 in the morning that Wagner himself informed him that his wife was no longer on the ship.

Emergency responders were soon radioed onto the scene and retrieved the body several hours later. Since Woods was with three other people on a yacht right before she slipped into the waters, the most obvious suspects are those three other people. So, if foul play is involved, it would most likely have been committed either by her husband Robert Wagner, the captain of the ship, Dennis Davern, or even fellow actor Christopher Walken.

Christopher Walken has been rather tight-lipped about the whole ordeal for decades. So much so, that many who are not aware of the story are shocked to learn that this megastar was even present on the night that Woods died.

Aiding in the perception of Walken's innocence, however, is the fact that both Captain Davern and Robert Wagner have insisted that Walken was asleep when Woods went missing.

So, unless there is some elaborate, bizarre conspiracy between all three men, it would seem that Walken most likely, really did sleep through the whole thing. And his silence is more of a pragmatic caution, than anything nefarious. Of these three men, it has always been Natalie's husband Robert Wagner who was the most likely suspect in a potential case of foul play.

And the suspicions swirling around Wagner just wouldn't go away. In 2018 in fact, the case, which had already been reopened, designated Wagner as a "person of interest." And as general interest, in this case, has grown, a rather stunning documentary about the whole episode came out in 2020, entitled "Natalie Wood: What Remains Behind." As a result, new questions are being asked, and the elderly Robert Wagner, now aged in his 90s, has found himself having to fight to prove his innocence once again.

In the End

As of this writing, there has been no trial and no conviction in this case. The death of Natalie Woods remains very much a mystery.

Remembering the Life and Tragic Death of Marvin Gaye

Who*:* Marvin Gaye
Where: Los Angeles, California
When: April 1, 1984
Suspect*:* Marvin Gaye Sr.
Conviction*:* 1984

Background Information

Marvin Gaye's last name was the original "Gay." He added the "e" at the end of his appellation after he became famous. He was the son of a preacher—Marvin Gay senior, and his wife Alberta Gay. Marvin Gaye grew up in the poorer neighborhoods of the greater Washington DC area. He developed a love of singing at a young age and often performed at his parents' Pentecostal Church.

Marvin Gaye's parents were often threadbare, and the hardship in his early life certainly wasn't an easy upbringing. Making matters worse, his father was borderline abusive, with harsh treatment of Marvin. Gaye would later recall how he would get beat by his Dad for the slightest perceived offense. During these tough times, it was always music that Marvin Gaye would fall back on, as his greatest source of comfort.

Marvin Gaye continued to sing like a young man, and by high school had participated in several singing groups. His grades weren't the best, however, and he ended up dropping out in 1956. At 17, he joined the military. Marvin Gaye didn't enjoy military life, however, and regretted the fact that he had enlisted, and actually feigned mental illness just to get discharged. He ended up getting a "general discharge."

Upon his arrival back in civilian life, he joined up with a local group called The Marquees. The vocals band began to tour all around the greater DC area, and after gaining some traction, managed to get signed to Okeh Records. After recording the single "Wyatt Earp" however, the group had little success and were subsequently taken off Okeh Records' roster.

Shortly thereafter, Marvin joined up with singer Harvey Fuqua to form the group Harvey Fuqua and the New Moon Glows. The group ultimately broke up in 1960 however, and Gaye and Fuqua both headed over to Detroit, Michigan. It was in Detroit that Gaye caught the attention of Motown's Berry Gordy—this led to Marvin signing with a Motown affiliate called Tamla.

It was with Tamla that he would release the album, "The Soulful Moods of Marvin Gaye." The album proved to be a failure, however, and Gaye was forced to resort to working as a studio session backup singer, in order to make any money. In between session work, Gaye did find some time to still record his own songs, however, and in 1963 he managed to craft his first hit, "Pride and Joy."

In the following year,1964, Gaye then released a live album, which contained another break-out hit, the song, "Can I Get a Witness." This was the first of many more hits to come throughout the 1960s. Most of these were romantic, feel-good tunes, but it was in 1971 that Gaye's most introspective piece, "What's Going On" would be released, and end up becoming his most well-known song. The subsequent "What's going On" album also became a best-seller.

His 1973 album, "Let's Get It On" was also a fan favorite, with the title track reaching number one on the charts. But even though he had reached the top, it was seemingly all downhill from there. And his next major album, "Here, My

Dear" was a commercial flop. Disappointed with the failure of his new music, Gaye began to descend into habitual drug use. These were disappointing times for Marvin Gaye for sure, but he wasn't about to give up.

In 1982, Gaye mounted a major comeback and his album "Midnight Love" managed to bring him another number one hit—"Sexual Healing". It turned out to be one of the most popular R & B tracks of the decade, and Gaye was awarded a Grammy for his efforts. Marvin Gaye was riding high on his newfound success, but it would all come crashing to a sudden, and abrupt halt, on April 1st, 1984, when he was shot and killed by his own father.

On that Day

On the 1st of April, 1984, Marvin Gaye was at his parents' house when an argument between himself and his father got out of hand. The argument apparently began between Marvin Sr. and his wife Alberta. The couple was arguing over an insurance policy when Marvin Gaye overheard. Marvin Gaye confronted his father and the verbal conflict quickly escalated into a physical one.

Alberta later testified that she saw her son Marvin punching and kicking Marvin Sr. Although she was certainly sad at the end result of her son being killed, she acknowledged that Marvin Gaye was probably a little out of control at this point. She later testified, "Marvin hit him. I shouted for him to stop, but he paid no attention to me. He gave my husband some hard kicks." It was after this physical altercation ran its course that the badly beaten Marvin Sr.

made the fateful decision to pull out a gun and shoot his own son.

Superstar singer Marvin Gaye was shot two times, the first bullet struck him right in the heart and the second hit him in the shoulder. Alberta again provides us with a gripping bit of testimony. She would later recall the incident, "I was standing about eight feet away from Marvin when my husband came to the door of the bedroom with his pistol. My husband didn't say anything, he just pointed the gun at Marvin. I screamed but it was very quick. He, my husband, shot—and Marvin screamed. I tried to run. Marvin slid down to the floor after the first shot."

Marvin Gaye was already dead after that first fateful shot, and the second was nothing more than malice and overkill on the part of his enraged father. Gaye was taken to the hospital but was declared dead upon arrival. If he had lived to see just one more day, he would have turned 45 years old.

The Investigation

At the outset of Marvin Gaye's death, investigators could quite easily conclude that Marvin had been killed by his own father. Marvin Gay Sr. himself admitted as much. Sadly, muttering at the crime scene about how he "didn't mean to do it." He didn't mean to do it he said—but investigators could safely conclude that he most certainly *did* do it. With such a clear case of guilt, there was really no need to pursue any other angles of investigation in this case. The investigation had essentially come to a close as soon as Marvin Gay Sr. was in custody.

The Suspect

The only suspect in the death of Marvin Gaye has always been his own father—*Marvin Gay Sr.* The only real question, in this case, was whether or not the crime was one that occurred in the heat of an argument, or if there was a more calculated motive for the killing. Both Alberta and Marvin Gay Sr.'s testimony closely corroborated each other, leaving little doubt as to who the suspect was. The crime scene evidence also clearly pointed to Marvin Gay Sr. as the prime suspect.

In the End

Marvin Gay Sr was initially hit with a "first-degree murder" charge for the killing. This was later reduced to that of "voluntary manslaughter." Marvin Gay Sr, ultimately pled "no contest" to voluntary manslaughter on the 20th of September, in 1984. His day of sentencing then arrived a couple of months later, on November 2nd.

In the end, Marvin Gay Sr was merely given a six-year suspended sentence, with an additional five years of probation attached. He never served one day in jail for the killing of his son. The judge no doubt must have taken into consideration the fact that Marvin Gay Sr, had a clean record, and the obvious nature of the crime.

It was horrible what the man had done to his own son, but by all accounts, it was a crime of passion. The man had been beaten pretty badly, and in a ballistic state of rage, he pulled the trigger—without thinking of all of the pain and death that he would cause superstar singer Marvin Gaye and lifelong sorrow for himself.

Marvin Gay Sr. would have to spend the rest of his life reflecting on the horror he had wrought. This alone must have been ample punishment for this man. Or as Marvin Sr. himself, reflected on his day of sentencing, "If I could bring him back, I would. I was afraid of him. I thought I was going to get hurt. I didn't know what was going to happen. I'm really sorry for everything that happened. I loved him. I wish he could step through this door right now. I'm paying the price now." Marvin Gay Sr. ended his days in a nursing home, where he passed away in 1998.

What Happened to Dorothy Stratten?

Who: Dorothy Stratten
Where: Hollywood, California
When: November 1981
Suspects: Paul Snider
Conviction: No Conviction/Suspect Deceased

Background Information

Dorothy Stratten came into this world on the 28th of February,1960. She was born and raised in Vancouver, Canada. She was still a teenager, scooping ice cream part-time at a Dairy Queen when she came into contact with a wannabe agent to the stars—Paul Snider. Snider began a relationship with the young woman and actually convinced her to have some naked photographs were taken, which he then subsequently sent off to "Playboy" in 1978. Dorothy was just 19 years old when "Playboy" came calling, leading to a long-term contract to work for them.

This led to Dorothy and Snider moving to Los Angeles, California. As Dorothy continued to work for the magazine and seek further advancement of her career, the two were married in 1979. Dorothy managed to get some roles in TV shortly thereafter, appearing on TV programs such as "Fantasy Island", and the science fiction classic—"Buck

Rogers". This in turn led to some parts in movies such as "Americathon" and the infamous "Skatetown, USA."

The relationship between Dorothy Stratten and Paul Snider in the meantime had begun to deteriorate, and it's said that Stratten started a relationship with director Peter Bogdanovich. It was Bogdanovich that would end up directing Dorothy Stratten's last film, "They All Laughed."

This was a comedy piece in which Dorothy Stratten starred alongside John Ritter, in the role of an "unhappy housewife" who falls in love with the character played by Ritter. It was while Stratten was working on this film, that Snider began to realize she was having an affair with Bogdanovich, and actually went so far as to hire a private detective to follow her movements.

A fact that stands as rather ironic, since part of the plot of "They All Laughed" involves detectives tracking the love affairs of the film's leading ladies. After Stratten got wind of what was happening, she informed Snider of her plans to leave him, and moved in with Bogdanovich, and made it clear that she was going to file for divorce. It was shortly after her intention was made known, that Dorothy Stratten would lose her life.

On that Day

Frustrated and enraged that his wife was slipping from his grasp, Paul Snider decided to take matters into his own hands. He made his way down to LA and actually began to quietly stalk Dorothy Stratten's every move. He eventually made his way right to Bogdanovich's residence where Stratten was staying. He would tool around in LA for a while before he made the fateful decision to kill Dorothy Stratten.

It was on August 13th, 1980 that he purchased a shotgun, and the following day, on the 14th, Snider arranged to have Stratten meet with him at the residence he was staying at in West Los Angeles. Paul Snider had two roommates at the time, but they decided to leave that morning so that the two former spouses could discuss the terms of their pending divorce.

The roommates would later return to find the couple closed up in Paul Snider's bedroom. Not sure what they might be up to, the roommates turned on a loud television, in order to keep to themselves and not interfere. It was actually Snider's private detective who grew concerned, and called up the roommates and urged them to go into the bedroom to check on the estranged couple. They entered around 11 pm, and it was then that they found the corpses of both Paul Snider and Dorothy Stratten—each slain from a gunshot wound.

The Investigation

The death of Dorothy Stratten was a shock to many, but perhaps none felt it more keenly than Playboy founder Hugh Hefner. Stratten had just been picked up as a rising star for Playboy, and as their first playmate of the year, for the first decade of the 1980's—Stratten had been touted as the "goddess of the new decade."

Hugh Hefner himself was said to have been pretty shook up by the incident. But his cold, calculated response to the news, didn't let on as such. At the time, he issued a statement that simply read, "The death of Dorothy Stratten comes as a shock to us all. As Playboy's Playmate of the Year, with a film and a television career of increasing importance, her professional future was a bright one. But equally sad to us is the fact that her loss takes from us all a very special member of the Playboy family."

This tepid response did hit all of the typical sad notes, but since it neglected to mention the horrific nature of Stratten's death, one might think she had simply died in her sleep. Nevertheless, the investigation into the deaths almost immediately settled upon the notion of a murder-suicide perpetrated by the disgruntled Paul Snider. The two had both died of a gunshot wound from Snider's shotgun, making this seem to be a clear enough possibility.

Additional speculation was generated from the fact that both of them were nude when they were killed. Had the couple engaged in intimacy just prior to the murder-suicide taking place? Although the details are not fully known, it has been suggested by investigators that perhaps Dorothy Stratten was sexually assaulted by Snider before he shot her, and then shot himself. A detail that also escapes most reports, is the fact that Stratten had a finger missing.

It's believed that it was after Stratten was dead that Snider—for reasons unknown—engaged in this slight dismemberment of her corpse. Autopsy results seem to suggest that Snider perished about half an hour after

Stratten. This gave Paul Snider several minutes to inflict additional post-mortem torment on Dorothy Stratten.

The Suspect

The main suspect has always been Dorothy Stratten's estranged husband, Paul Snider.

In the End

With the main suspect deceased, there was no trial or conviction in this case. Stratten was buried at the Westwood Memorial Park Cemetery in Los Angeles.

The studios refused to release her last movie "They All Laughed" considering the gruesome murder of Stratten. The movie was released in 1988 by Bogdanovich personally but it was a total flop that almost ruined him.

Snider's family got their hands on Stratten's estate after suing for it as Snider and Stratten were still married, making Snider her only beneficiary.

The Tragic Case of Selena

Who: Selena Quintanilla Perez
Where: San Antonio, Texas
When: March 1995
Suspect: Yolanda Saldivar
Conviction: 1995

Background Information

Superstar Selena Quintanilla Perez was born in the town of Lake Jackson, in the state of Texas, on the 16th of April,1971. She was the daughter of a music producer and business entrepreneur by the name of Abraham Quintanilla, and his wife, Marcella. Her father realized that Selena had musical talent early on in her life, and encouraged her to hone her musical skills.

It was her Dad who became her first manager and put her in her first music group—*Selena y Los Dinos*. Selena seemed to be a rising star, but her grades in school began to suffer. Her father ended up letting her drop out completely, after the eighth grade, so that she could finish school through a home-based, correspondence course, which she completed successfully at the age of 17. Selena's first big break came in 1989 when she was signed for EMI Latin Records.

It was with this record company that Selena produced the self-titled record—"Selena". The album wasn't exactly a smash hit, but Selena did see some traction on the music charts. This album was followed by the 1990's "Ven Conmigo" which gained a wide following in Mexico. It was around this time that Selena got the attention of a woman named Yolanda Saldivar.

Ms. Saldivar actually contacted her father and proposed the idea of starting a "fan club" for Selena based out of San Antonio, Texas, in order to better get the word out about Selena's music. Mr. Quintanilla thinking it a fairly reasonable idea, gave her the green light to do so. Thanks to her efforts, Yolanda not only increased Selena's recognition but also became quite close to Selena herself.

Someone else who became close with Selena at this time was a band member—Chris Perez. Selena's father was not happy when he got word of the romance, fearing that it could derail Selena's career. He told the couple to stop seeing each other. Perez, a gifted bass guitarist, ended up leaving the band, but he continued to see Selena behind the scenes, culminating in the couple secretly eloping to get married. They were wed in secret, on the 2nd of April, in 1992.

Mr. Quintanilla was upset, but eventually came around to the idea, and not only accepted the marriage but brought Chris Perez back into the band. It was on the heels of all of these developments that Selena cut her next record— "Entre a Mi Mundo". This album was a smashing success, reaching number one on the US Billboard Regional Mexican Albums chart.

In 1993, she then followed up this success with a live album, named simply "LIVE!" The album won a Grammy for Best Mexican American Album. It was around this time that Yolanda Saldivar, the former director of Selena's fan club, had weaseled her way into becoming Selena's manager. Soon Yolanda's world would begin to unravel, however, when in January of 1995, Selena's father Quintanilla, would get tipped off that Yolanda was ripping off fans who had paid membership fees, and pocketing the money for herself.

Mr. Quintanilla warned Yolanda that if she did not come up with an explanation for what was happening, he would file a police report. He told Selena in the meantime, to stay away from Yolanda. Selena however, found it hard to part company with Yolanda, who otherwise seemed totally devoted to Selena's career. It was on March 31st, 1995, that Selena met up with Yolanda at a hotel, apparently in an attempt to resolve some of these pressing problems once and for all.

On that Day

On March 31st, 1995, Selena was found shot to death in a motel. The previous night, she and her husband had arrived at the motel together. But there was a third party involved— Yolanda, Selena's manager. A middle-aged, domineering woman, Yolanda had been calling the shots for Selena for some time, and she was meeting up with her at the motel, supposedly to hammer out some pending details in Selena's latest contracts.

But at some point, Yolanda pulled out a gun and shot Selena Perez right in the middle of her back. With ruptured arteries spilling blood, Selena was mortally wounded, yet she still struggled with the last of her fading energy and managed to run out of the motel room, and down the hall, only to fall to in a heap—all of her strength gone—as she fell to the floor of the hotel lobby.

The Investigation

Just before she died, Selena had named Yolanda as her killer, and if there wasn't any further doubt, shortly thereafter Yolanda herself came charging into the lobby waving a gun and calling the dying Selena a "bitch."

The Suspect

Shortly after Selena's death, the main suspect, Yolanda, fled the scene in a pickup truck but was tracked down by police shortly thereafter. Yolanda feigning suicidal ideation, put the gun to her head while the police and FBI negotiated with her for several hours. At various points during this ordeal, she seemed about ready to comply with officers, but as soon as one approached her car, she would put the gun to her head, or even in her mouth, indicating that if the police came any closer, she would shoot.

Finally, however, she was convinced to put the gun down and ceased taking herself hostage. She was taken into police custody. There was no further major incident, but Yolanda was so emotionally panicked, sobbing and crying, that the police put a coat over her, apparently to shield her from onlookers.

The public was indeed enraged, and crowds had already swarmed around the area that had been cordoned off by police. Even after Yolonda was put behind bars, fans began to wait outside the jail, thinking that perhaps she might make bail. And if she did, they apparently didn't have her best interest in mind.

In the End

Just prior to being put on trial, authorities placed Yolanda under protective custody to safeguard her both from herself and from others who might do her harm. Due to the sensational nature of the crime and the outpouring of grief for the victim, the sheriff was quoted as saying, "We don't want to take any chances, because there are some people who are wanting to retaliate."

Former Selena manager, Yolanda Saldivar was put on trial for Selena's death in October of 1995. Just a few days after the trial had commenced, the jury rather quickly deliberated, and Yolanda was found guilty as charged and handed a sentence of life in prison with the chance of potential parole in 2025.

Lana Clarkson
Who Killed the Barbarian
Queen?

Who: Lana Clarkson
Where: Hollywood, California
When: 2003
Suspect: Phil Spector
Conviction: 2005

Background Information

Lana Clarkson was born in 1962 and grew up in Sonoma County, California. After high school, she moved to southern California, and then Los Angeles, where she began work as a model and sought gigs as an actress. Her first big break came when she landed a small part for "Fast Times at Ridgemont High." After this, she landed a part in the classic 1983 gangster film "Scarface."

It was shortly after this that she was recruited by filmmaker Roger Corman, to star in his epic sword and sorcery movie, "Deathstalker." In this piece, she starred as the romantic lead opposite the main character. This film led to another. His next gig was the infamous 1985 flick, "Barbarian Queen." In which Lana Clarkson played—you guessed it—a Barbarian Queen!

Many would regard these features as B-movies, so it is with some irony that a couple of years after this, in 1987, she took part in a science-fiction satire entitled, "Amazon Women on the Moon." Shortly thereafter, Lana reprised her Barbarian Queen role, to appear in "Barbarian Queen II: The Empress Strikes Back."

Her next film was the 1990's "The Haunting of Morella." This was a film with a horror/supernatural plot that had Lana delving into the occult to contact the soul of a sorceress who was killed during the Salem Witch Trials. Although her films were largely written off by the critics as being a bit cheesy, and in the realm of B-movies, she had cultivated a large fan following and was often invited to comic cons to reprise her barbarian warrior roles.

Throughout the 1990s she made several more television and film appearances. By the early 2000s however, her career had slowed down considerably. She attempted to market some of her memorabilia and previous work on a website, and when that didn't bring in enough cash, she actually resorted to getting a part-time job as a waitress at the House of Blues in West Hollywood, California.

It was certainly quite a fall for a woman who had previously enjoyed the life of an actress on demand. She had seen the bright lights of Hollywood only to have them rapidly dim before her eyes. It was as she was struggling to regain her footing that her life would come to a sudden and abrupt end.

On that Day

It was on the 3rd of February, 2003 that veteran actress Lana Clarkson's dead body was discovered at the residence of legendary studio genius Phil Spector. Phil was well known of course, for his work with the Beatles and other famous musicians during his heyday in the 1960s and 1970s.

Phil a frequent patron at the House of Blues, had gotten to know Lana Clarkson after she started working there. It was on that February day that Lana left her job at the restaurant in the company of Phil Spector, to further hang out with him at his residence. They were driven by Spector's personal chauffeur, who dutifully remained outside, seated in the vehicle while Spector and Lana went indoors.

Some time had passed before the chauffeur suddenly heard what sounded like a gun going off from somewhere in the residence. The chauffeur then spotted Phil Spector, running out of the house with a gun in his hand. Spector apparently, not trying to hide anything, muttered something along the lines of "I think I just shot her."

The Investigation

Investigators didn't have to look far for Lana Clarkson's killer, and according to Phil Spector's chauffeur, he had admitted to the crime. But upon being taken into custody, Phil Spector began to change his story. He told police that he believed that Lana Clarkson had succumbed to an "accidental suicide."

Phil Spector tried to say that Lana Clarkson was playing around with his gun and tried to kiss it. According to Phil, it was then that the gun went off. Police weren't ready to believe this version of events, however, and soon Phil was being brought up on charges for Lana's murder.

The Suspect

Phil Spector was true, the only suspect believed to have been involved in Lana Clarkson's death.

In the End

Phil Spector was first put on trial in the Fall of 2007, but this trial was overturned after it resulted in a hung jury. A new trial was then convened on October 20th, 2008. After a long, dramatic ordeal, Spector was ultimately found guilty as charged on April 13th, 2009. This resulted in him being given 19 years to a life sentence. Phil Spector would ultimately finish out his term by way of his own death when he perished from Covid-19 in 2021.

The Troubling Saga of Robert Blake and Bonny Lee Bakley

Who: Bonny Lee Bakley
Where: Hollywood, California
When: May 2001
Suspect: Robert Blake
Conviction: No Conviction - Main Suspect Acquitted

Background Information

Bonny Lee Bakley was born in Morristown, New Jersey on June 7th, 1956. As a teenager, Bonny moved to New York to pursue acting. It didn't work out, however, and by her early 20s, she had been married, and divorced two times, with several kids in between. Strapped for cash, during the 1980s, Bonny resorted to regularly peddling smut and scamming gullible men to make a living.

She began posting want ads in the "lonely hearts" section of local newspapers. Any men desperate enough to respond would inevitably get scammed out of some money by Bonny. In those pre-internet days, she was also known to send erotic pictures of herself and others to her clients in the mail. Bonny's less-than respectable enterprises, and involvement with a series of sketchy characters, eventually got her in trouble.

In 1989 for example, she was put in jail for drug possession, and in 1995 she was hit up with charges of check fraud. For the check fraud incident, she was fined $1000 and actually made to labor on a penal farm for restitution. Along with Bonny's attempts to scam lonely, obscure men, she also desired to reel in one of the stars. She confided in those who knew her that she desired to get into a relationship with a Hollywood celebrity.

Someone rich and famous of course would be able to open up doors for her that the average Joe just wouldn't be able to. It was with this in mind, that she first ran into Robert Blake at a "jazz club"' in the year 1999. It was shortly into their relationship that Bonny discovered that she was pregnant. Using this baby as her ticket to getting hitched to a star, Bonny suggested marriage. Robert Blake agreed but made her place her signature on a prenuptial agreement.

The agreement was more than a little odd. It stipulated that Bonny had to have "written permission" for anyone to visit Robert Blake's ranch house and that if one of them were to initiate a divorce, custody of the baby would automatically go to the other. The couple wed in November of 2000. It was a low-budget affair, that Robert Blake apparently didn't even dress up for. He was seen wearing his casual, everyday clothes, whereas Bonny had on a full-blown wedding gown.

Very few people attended the event, but Blake was sure to have at least one person on hand—his personal attorney. After getting married, although Bonny and the baby moved onto the property, they stayed in the bungalow guest house, rather than under the same roof with Robert Blake.

Robert Blake rather than having a wife seemed to have simply brought an estranged dependent onto his property.

Shortly into this arrangement, Blake apparently began to seriously wonder what this woman was doing in her free time. The paranoid Blake actually hired a private detective to look into her background. The detective discovered that Bonny Lee Bakley was still actively scamming other men out of money, even after marrying Robert Blake. It wasn't long after this revelation that Bonny's life would come to an end.

On that Day

Bonny Lee Bakley had dinner with her husband Robert Blake on May 4th, 2001. They were dining at an upmarket Italian bistro called Vitello's. Blake was a regular at the joint—so regular in fact, that they ended up naming a menu item after him. Consisting of spinach, tomato, and pasta, his favorite meal was dubbed the "fusilli a la Robert Blake."

Blake was seated in the back of the restaurant that night, and after ordering their usual fare, the couple dined to the tunes of a nearby piano player. It was sometime in between eating and leaving that Blake was seen going to the restroom. A patron would later clearly recall seeing the actor "vomiting into a trash can" and "pulling at his hair" as he began "mumbling to himself."

This seemed to be an obvious sign of distress, and after leaving the restroom, he continued to appear sickly. Yet, Blake had not drunk any alcohol, nor did his food seem to be amiss. Whatever was bothering Blake, he kept it to himself. After paying for their meal, the couple quietly left, leaving patrons to wonder to themselves what was wrong with the megastar.

But after he and Bonny got back to the car, Blake realized he had forgotten something. Did he leave his keys? His wallet maybe? No—nothing like that. He had left his gun behind. Not the typical item a patron simply forgets and leaves behind. But this was apparently the case. Realizing his gun had been left behind, Blake told his wife Bonny to hang tight, while he went back to retrieve it.

According to Robert Blake's version of events, it was after he returned to the car that he found Bonny deceased, with a bullet in her brain. She was "slumped over" and bleeding profusely, and according to Blake, he had no idea who had just killed his wife. Did some random sociopath just happen upon Bonny and pull the trigger? Or did an old enemy suddenly come out of the woodwork? Blake's account may seem hard to believe—but stranger things have happened.

At any rate, Blake's response was a little unusual, to say the least. Instead of immediately calling the police or 911, he took off on foot, to the nearby residence of a buddy of his, Hollywood director—Sean Stanek. It was through Stanek that authorities would be called to the scene, and the whole world subsequently heard the news of this strange and horrific event.

Strangely enough, Blake was missing in action for the rest of this tragic event. To be sure, it was already clear that Bonny had passed, but nevertheless, most husbands would have been present when their slain wife's body was transported from the scene. But not Blake. Instead, he continued to make himself rather scarce.

Blake would get media attention, however, when he himself was put in the hospital. According to this attorney, Blake was "in an absolute state of shock." This is perhaps an exaggerated version of events since the real culprit was his high blood pressure. But that's not to say that Blake wasn't rattled by recent events. He most certainly was.

The Investigation

The investigation into Bonny's death heated up on the day following her murder, on May 5th, when the LAPD made the decision to raid Robert Blake's residence. Blake owned a ranch house just a few minutes from the same Vitello restaurant where Bonny and Blake had dined just prior to her death. There was an additional bungalow on the residence, which investigators would learn, was what Bonny Lee Bakely used as her primary home.

On the 5th, after approaching the main compound, police banged on the front door, and after a moment Robert Blake came out. He was given a search warrant, so he stepped aside, and allowed the investigators to do their thing. During the course of the search, detectives on the scene interviewed Robert Blake, and at one point the interview allegedly got pretty intense, with the questioner basically suggesting that Blake was the killer.

It was at this point that Blake terminated the interview, and shortly thereafter he hired a powerful and experienced lawyer by the name of Harland Braun. Braun was an experienced criminal defense attorney and famous for working on the infamous Rodney King, police brutality case. But although Robert Blake wasn't talking—apparently the walls were. The words "I'm not going down for this!" were found scrawled right across one of Robert Blake's bathroom walls.

It was shortly after this discovery that Robert Blake was given a "gunpowder residue test." This is a test that is conducted in order to see if someone still has the residue of gunpowder on their hands, indicating that they have recently fired a weapon. The tests proved to be unhelpful, however, because it was discovered that Blake had been out target practicing just before Bonny's death. Any gun powder on his hands, therefore, could not be deemed as proof of murder, since no one could establish exactly when or where the residue may have gotten on Blake.

The Suspect

Pretty soon after Bonny's death, investigators began looking into Robert Blake as the number one suspect for the crime. Blake, in fact, was basically accused of being the killer by detectives from day one. As soon as he was made aware that he was indeed a suspect, Robert Blake lawyered up. His lawyer Harland Braun, openly criticized the investigators for having tunnel vision and zeroing in on Blake and Blake alone.

Braun pointed out that due to Bonny's previous swindles, there could be a wide variety of other potential suspects lurking in the shadows that the narrow-minded investigators were refusing to look into. It was argued that out of the countless men that Bonny had scammed over the years, there were several potential suspects with an ax to grind if investigators would just look into it. This was denied by investigators, but Robert Blake was placed into custody on charges of murder on April 18th, 2002, all the same.

In the End

After being arrested for murder Robert Blake was hauled off to prison to wait to stand trial. Unlike other celebrities who managed to get their "get out of jail free" card early, Blake would stay behind bars for a full year before he was able to post his one-and-a-half million-dollar bail. His trial then began on December 20th, 2004. The prosecution tried to paint Blake as a man who was willing to stoop to murder in order to get himself out of a terrible marriage that he was forced into with Bonny.

Not only that, they were able to fill in the jury on the long history Bonny had in sending out salacious letters and photos to men for her "lonely hearts" scam. These letters had her speaking at length on a wide variety of erotic themes, and it seemed that the activity continued well into her marriage with Robert Blake. The argument was made that Bonny's killer could have been any one of these men that she led on, and scammed money out of, with the twisted games that she played.

At the same time, the defense presented a powerful argument for Blake's innocence, pointing out that there was no tangible evidence that directly linked him to the crime. Blake was ultimately acquitted of the charges on March 16th, 2005. Later that Fall, however, Blake was found "liable" in a civil suit and was forced to shell out some 30 million dollars in compensation, which was then subsequently reduced upon appeal to 15 million. Bonny's killer remains free to this day.

Rebecca Schaeffer
Slain by a Deranged Fan

Who: Rebecca Schaeffer
Where: West, Hollywood, California
When: July 1989
Suspects: H
Conviction: 1989

Background Information

Rebecca Schaeffer was born on the 6th of November, 1967, the daughter of Benson and Danna Schaeffer. She got the acting bug early on in life, and by her teens, was modeling for magazines and appearing in TV commercials. Then in 1984, she convinced her Mom and Dad to let her relocate to New York to further her career. It was shortly thereafter that she managed to land a role in the popular soap opera—*One Life to Live.* This was an acting gig that lasted for several months.

Her next big breakthrough role came in 1984 when she was given the part of "Patti"
in the sitcom "My Sister Sam." She played the little sister of the title character named "Samantha (Sam)." The series exceeded expectations at first, but when head honchos at the studio decided to abruptly change the time slot from Tuesday to Saturday, the audience didn't seem to appreciate this fact and neglected to tune in. As a result, the previously popular show's ratings crashed and the TV series was ultimately canceled and taken off the air.

Rebecca Schaeffer would pick up roles in the film shortly thereafter, however, including a piece called "Scenes from the Class Struggle in Beverly Hills." Little did Schaeffer know that there was an obsessed fan who was stalking her—a fan who would eventually end her life. This fan—Robert John Bardo—had written to Schaeffer in 1987 and she was kind enough to write him back. But that wasn't enough for this misguided admirer, and by 1989 he would show up—right at her door.

On that Day

It was on the 18th of July, 1989, that a 19-year-old guy by the name of Robert John Bardo, suddenly showed up at Shaeffer's West Hollywood apartment. He had figured out her home address by hiring a private investigator. Once in the area, he then wandered around until locals helped him further pinpoint the exact location. Schaeffer had been getting ready to try out for the film "The Godfather Part III" and was actually waiting for a draft of the film's screenplay to be brought to her.

So due to this unfortunate coincidence, when John Bardo just happened to ring her doorbell, she eagerly answered the door expecting it to be someone from the set. But the person who greeted her was not a Hollywood representative with a freshly printed script, but rather a deranged fan waving the letter that Schaefer had been kind enough to send him previously. The stalker, John Bardo waved the letter in the air as if it were proof of her undying love—for a man that she had never met and knew absolutely nothing about.

Rebecca Schaeffer was startled by the odd stranger, but after a few words with him, she tried, as politely as possible, to ask him to leave. John did peaceably leave at this time, heading off to a local restaurant to get something to eat. He returned right after that, however, and again Rebecca Schaeffer answered the door.

According to John Bardo, she had a "cold look on her face." She was no doubt displeased to be disturbed by this strange and frightening man, yet Bardo, not understanding how he was bothering the young woman, took offense to her "coldness."

It was at this point that Bardo, without saying another word, took out his gun and shot Rebecca Schaeffer right in the heart. John Bardo apparently was determined to either have Schaeffer for himself or to kill her and make sure no one else did. As Rebecca Schaeffer fell to the ground, Bardo himself would later admit that the one word that escaped from her mouth was "Why?" Yes, in the face of such senseless violence, we would all ask that same question.

The Investigation

John Bardo fled the scene after killing actress Rebecca Schaeffer, but the crazed 19-year-old didn't get very far. He was found the next day, literally "running through traffic." After a few phone calls to the police, he was tracked down, arrested, and thrown in jail. As soon as he was brought into police custody, Bardo readily admitted to murdering Rebecca Schaefer.

The Suspects

After John Bardo's confession, it was clear that he was the killer. There were no other suspects in this case.

In the End

Since John Bardo confessed to Rebecca Schaeffer's murder, he was given a bench trial. Upon his conviction, he was subsequently sentenced to serve the rest of his life in prison. He's still behind bars to this very day.

Pondering the Fate of Sharon Tate

Who: Sharon Tate
Where: California
When: August 1969
Suspects: Charles Manson, Tex Watson, Susan Atkins, Patricia Krenwinkle, Linda Kasabian
Conviction: 1969

Background Information

Although Sharon Tate is no doubt known for her death than her life, it would be remiss not to mention the brief acting career that she had before the unthinkable occurred. Prior to her emergence in Hollywood, Tate began life in Dallas Texas, where she was born in 1943. Her father was a military man—Colonel Paul Tate—and shortly after her birth, her Dad's career took her far and wide.

Tate in the meantime blossomed into a beauty and participated in several beauty pageants. It was when her father had her shipped out with him to LA, however, that she began to consider pursuing acting. She was just a high schooler when she first began to audition for parts. This led to a few spots in TV commercials. This then led to more parts in TV and even a few movies.

Tate had met film-maker Roman Polanski in 1966, in the meantime, and through him was very nearly given a part on one of his latest films—"Rosemary's Baby". At the last minute, however, she was passed over by another actress. Nevertheless, this was a horror film that involved much occultic imagery, and the fact that she would later be killed in what seemed to be a cult ritual, almost reminiscent of the happenings in this very film, would create much innuendo and speculation.

On that Day

It was on August 9th, 1969, that Winifred Chapman, the cleaning lady, showed up at the Hollywood residence of famed director Roman Polanski, to find much more of a mess than she had bargained for. Greeting her right on the front lawn of the home was a dead man, sprawled out, right there on the grass, with blood pooling all around him. Winifred didn't know the guy, but his name was Wojtek Frykowski, an occasional visitor to the residence.

The killers behind this crime scene quite clearly wanted attention, and rather than hide their deeds, they showcased them for all to see. After encountering this first victim, the horrified cleaning lady then turned to the front door to find that the word, "PIG" was scrawled across the door in blood. Inside the residence, things were even worse, for here the body of Sharon Tate was found in a terrible state.

Tate was pregnant at the time of her death, and the fiends that killed here were apparently quite aware of this fact, as her pregnant belly had been mercilessly torn apart, along with several slash wounds on her throat, breasts, and other parts of her person, from which fountains of blood had flowed. The violence that was inflicted on this poor woman was beyond belief; besides being stabbed and hacked to death, she also had a rope wrapped around her throat.

Again, as if all of this were some sort of full-on macabre display, the rope actually led to another victim—Jay Sebring. The other end of the rope wrapped around Sharon's throat was actually wrapped around Jay's throat. It's unclear whether this was done after they were both dead or not, but Jay had been subjected to a litany of assault as well.

He was shot in the back, but also stabbed multiple times. Another victim was found in another section of the property's yard—a lady who was also subjected to multiple stab wounds, leaving a pool of blood behind. The cleaning lady, Winifred Chapman, who stumbled onto this scene was either incredibly brave or just completely shellshocked. Most would have probably run out of that horror show as fast as they could, but Ms. Chapman dutifully checked the entire house for survivors. Realizing there were none, she finally called the cops.

The Investigation

Investigators on the scene of the Tate murders almost immediately surmised that there must be some sort of cult group at work. The way that the victims had been posed, and the sheer brutality of it all, just seemed to scream something more than your typical break-in. This appeared to be the work of a vicious and sinister group of cultists.

Roman Polanski's agent, Bill Tennant in the meantime had the terrible responsibility of reaching out to Roman—who was away in London at the time— to let him know the terrible news. Having a hard time finding the right words to use, Bill finally settled on saying, "Roman, there's been a disaster at the house. Sharon is dead. And Wojtek. And Gibby and Jay. There's been a slaughter."

It was indeed a disaster of epic proportions and calling it a slaughter was probably one of the best descriptions he could have made. Roman Polanski immediately returned to

LA, where he had to not only deal with this personal loss but the media circus that had ensued.

The Suspects

Besides the notion being floated that a cult was involved, investigators also zeroed in on two other potential persons of interest. Roman Polanski of course, was a prime suspect, simply because it was his house, and the victims were people associated with him. Also, the fact that he just happened to be out when all this happened, created a potential scenario of someone skipping town so that a hired hitman could go to work.

Another suspect interestingly enough was one of the victims—the slain Wojtek Frykowski. Since Wojtek had himself been killed in such a horrific fashion, he obviously wasn't considered the actual murderer. Nevertheless, when it was found that Wojtek was a drug dealer and was routinely dropping off drugs at the residence, this of course could not be ignored. As such, police looked into the lives of both Wojtek Frykowski and Roman Polanski at the outset of the investigation.

This was an early angle, but after LA was rocked by more killings that seemed to mimic the Tate murders, investigators changed their trajectory once again back to the notion that the main suspects were most likely part of a cult, committing ritual murders.

This angle led them right to the Charles Manson cult. Investigators took the cult leader and several of his disciples into custody and determined that they were indeed the prime suspects of this case.

The cult "family" that Charles Manson led, was indeed a strange and diabolical bunch. Manson's followers were deluded with both drugs and Manson's own incredible knack for brainwashing. Manson had so warped the minds of his followers, that cult members had nothing but good things to say about Manson. In fact, one of them who was hauled into custody was quoted as saying, "Charlie is in love with us and we are all in love with Charlie."

So in love, in fact, to commit murder at his command? This was the conclusion that investigators ultimately came to. The clearly defined perpetrators of the crime would come to be listed as Manson disciples: Charles "Tex" Watson, Susan Atkins, Patricia Krenwinkle, and Linda Kasabian.

It would later come out that the murder spree began when Tex Watson made his way through a window, into the home, and then crept up to the front door to let his three accomplices in with him. Watson then converged on Wojtek Frykowski who was sleeping on a couch in the living room. Watson poked the slumbering man with his gun and hissed, "Get up!" Frykowski awakened to see his gun-wielding assailant and muttered, "Who...?" Watson shouted, "Shut up! Shut up or you're a dead man!"

No matter how much Wojtek Frykowski may have complied, however, his fate was most likely already determined regardless. At one point, he was indeed able to finish a sentence, however, and managed to ask, "Who are you?"

To which Watson hauntingly replied, "I'm the Devil and I'm here to do the Devil's business."

Wojtek Frykowski was then tied up and the three women intruders went to a guest room where Abigail Folger was slumbering. Atkins woke the girl up with a knife to her throat and shouted for her to "go into the living room." And promised, "Just do as I say and you won't get hurt." Since this girl was mercilessly slaughtered, this was obviously not true. Sadly, cooperating wouldn't end up doing her any good.

Nevertheless, she meekly complied and was led to the living room where the tied-up Frykowski had been left. Atkins then found the room where Sharon Tate and Jay Sebring were and used a bit of subterfuge to get their attention. As a testament to the fact that this residence had a lot of people coming and going, Atkins was able to act like she was the house guest everyone forgot.

She entered the room as if she were a regular, and concocted a story to get their attention, shouting, "Hurry, they need you in the living room! Something terrible has happened!" What she really meant was "something terrible" *was about to happen.* The ruse worked, however, and Tate and Sebring rushed off to the living room. They were greeted by the sight of Tex Watson who had leveled his gun on the tied-up Frykowski, and Patricia Krenwinkle who was pointing her knife at Abigail Folger.

In shock, Sharon is said to have exclaimed, "What is this?" Sharon was perhaps a bit wiser than the rest, because rather than cooperating, she seemed to realize what was at stake, turned around, and tried to run. She was stopped midstride, however, by that same mystery house guest that had previously feigned distress—Susan Atkins—who was wielding a mean-looking knife, pointed right at her pregnant stomach.

Tex Watson then commanded all of them, "Over to the fireplace!" Jay Sebring initially tried to resist, muttering, "You people are crazy." Prompting the tied-up Frykowski to exclaim, "For God's sake, do what he says! He told me he'll shoot me if you don't do as he says!" Little did Wojtek Frykowski know that Jay Sebring either fighting back or running to get help, was the best shot that any of them would have to stay alive.

Unfortunately, Jay Sebring suspended his fight or flight response, however, and just like Frykowski and Abigail, he bowed down like a meek lamb for the impending slaughter. All four victims then went over to the fireplace as directed. Watson then ordered all of them, "On your stomachs!"

Obviously, a pregnant woman like Sharon Tate would not be able to do such a thing without courting the risk of injuring her baby, yet they still insisted she does as instructed. Sebring then provoked Watson's cruelty, by daring to suggest, "Be reasonable for Christ's sake. The woman'll hurt herself!"

Tex Watson, not one to enjoy correction, didn't like this one bit. The psychopath snapped, "Don't talk to me about Christ!" He then surprised them all by shooting Sebring right in the back. So much for "cooperate and you won't get hurt," right? It's quite clear that the best thing Tate and her friends could have done was to have fought like hell from the very beginning, now with Jay Sebring shot, and Wojtek Frykowski tied up, Abigail Folger and a pregnant Sharon Tate were left to deal with these fiends on their own.

Perhaps even then they still had a shot, if they could have summoned the courage to suddenly charge through their assailants. But sadly, there was no last-minute attempt to fight or take flight. In fact, as Jay Sebring lay dying, there would only be more compliance. At one point Watson demanded money, and the tied-up Wojtek Frykowski actually called out Abigail Folger direct. When Watson asked, "Who's got money?" Frykowski nodded toward Abigail and informed, "She does."

Singled out like this, Abigail Folger was forced to admit that she had some cash in her purse, which she had left in her bedroom. Watson then had Atkins retrieve it. But if Wojtek Frykowski thought that handing over Abigail's cash would end this nightmare, and allow three out of four of them to live, he was mistaken.

Frykowski was tied up with a towel so that Watson could use the rope for another purpose. Showing how demented he was, he tied it around the already dead Sebring's throat. He then tied loops around both Abigail and Sharon's throats, and while everyone meekly watched, he threw the other end over a beam. Watson then yanked on the rope over the beam, pulling on Sharon and Abigail so hard that they were forced to their feet. Watson then told the truth for a change, as he announced, "You're all going to die!"

With everyone restrained and subdued, Watson leaped upon Jay Sebring's corpse, stabbing it multiple times, causing blood to splatter everywhere. Watson then pointed the knife at the restrained Sharon Tate, and told her, "You will die like a pig!" It was only then, that Wojtek Frykowski, finally realizing that there would be no reasoning with these murderous psychopaths, finally began to fight back.

He started struggling to get his hands out of the towel, but by then this feeble show of resistance had come far too late. His efforts to struggle free were noticed, prompting Watson to shout, "Kill him!" Atkins then leaped upon him with a knife in hand. He was able to dodge the blow and had freed his hands enough to grab her arm, but a knife still managed to sink into his leg and side.

Tex Watson then intervened and pistol-whipped Wojtek Frykowski in the back of the head. The handle of the pistol actually broke, and despite the trauma to his cranium, Frykowski running on pure adrenaline got to his feet and began stumbling toward the front door. Watson still wielding the pistol, busted handle and all, managed to squeeze off a couple of shots, hitting Wojtek Frykowski in the back.

Nevertheless, Frykowski still made his way through the door before collapsing on the porch. While this was going on, Abigail Folger had managed to pull herself free from the rope that had been wrapped around her throat and began running down the hall.

Watson realized she was getting away and ordered his female assailants to "Get her!" It was Manson disciple

Patricia Krenwinkle who subdued the fleeing woman by leaping on her with a knife, plunging it into her back.

Tex Watson then joined the fray and stabbed her in the stomach. Sharon Tate, seeing what was happening, began screaming. This brief distraction apparently allowed Abigail to get up, and though badly wounded, she made one last desperate dash down the hall, through Sharon's bedroom, and then outside to the swimming pool. Watson was close on her heels, however, and after tackling her, began stabbing her.

His partner Patricia Krenwinkle then joined in, stabbing as well. Abigail Folger had no chance at this point, and even after she was dead, the demented duo continued stabbing. After satiating their bloodlust, Tex Watson and Patricia Krenwinkle returned to the living room to find Sharon Tate attempting to take the rope off of her neck. Manson disciple, Susan Atkins was there standing guard but was apparently oblivious to these developments.

Infuriated that she might get away, Watson gave the order, "Kill her!" Atkins leaped up, and halfheartedly tried to tackle Sharon to the ground, but ended up having Tate fall on top of her. Watson growled, "I said to kill her!"

But Susan Atkins pinned under the weight of Sharon Tate, either couldn't—or didn't want to proceed. Sharon in the meantime was sobbing, "My baby—I want my baby!" Watson, as if on the evil and demented cue, then stabbed Sharon right in the stomach. It was at this point, with her baby most likely dead, that Sharon Tate seemed to give up. And she didn't resist as Atkins stabbed her in the chest.

Tate falling to the side in a bloody heap, Susan Atkins then had the grisly idea of cutting her baby out of her stomach.

After several stabs and hacks, however, Atkins was unable to do so. It was then that Watson ordered all of the Manson disciples to make their exit. Upon leaving they found Frykowski's corpse, and Watson made sure to stab him a few more times for good measure. Tex Watson then recalled that Manson wanted them to leave a specific calling card.

It was then Susan Atkins who took a bloody towel and used it to write "PIG" on the front door, in blood. Atkins then left one last finishing touch, by going into the house and tying the rope tightly around the throats of Sharon Tate and Sebring, leaving them in this grisly pose of being tied together. The group then made their exit.

They wouldn't get far, however, and it wasn't long before Manson and his disciples were in police custody, being arrested in December of 1969. What we know of what transpires, comes from their own testimony. Disciple Susan Atkins, in particular, would recall the entire event in great detail. Much of what we know about what transpired, is from her own testimony.

In the End

Manson and his cohorts were put on trial in 1970. Even though Manson did not personally kill anyone at the Tate residence, he was found to have ordered the hit, making him the mastermind behind it. This landed him the death sentence. The sentence was later commuted to life imprisonment. Charles Manson passed away of natural causes in his prison cell in 2017.

Dominique Dunne
A Life Lost to an Abusive and
Controlling Man

Who: Dominque Dunne
Where: West Hollywood, California
When: October 1982
Suspect: John Sweeney
Conviction: 1982

Background Information

Dominique Dunne came into this world on the 23rd of
November, in the year 1959.
The daughter and namesake of journalist, Dominick Dunne,
she grew up in California, and by her teens was already on
a course set for stardom. She was appearing in both TV
and film by the late 1970s. One of her big breaks came in
1979 when she worked on the made-for-TV movie, "Diary of
a Teenage Hitchhiker."

Capitalizing on this experience, Dominique continued to
expand her resume in Hollywood, seeking bigger and better
roles. And by 1982 she had become a household name
through her work in the film "Poltergeist." In this iconic
movie, Dominique played the part of the daughter of Steven
and Diane Freeling—a California couple experiencing
ghostly poltergeist activity. This was Dominique's debut on
not just the national—*but international* stage—showcasing
her acting talent for the whole world to see.

161

This film in all likelihood should have been her springboard to future superstardom. And good things were indeed coming through the pipeline, such as her work in the epic TV mini-series "V" which depicted a deceptive alien civilization, attempting to seize the Earth through subterfuge.

For this science fiction masterpiece, Dunne was to play the part of "Robin Maxwell." She was now quite used to taking on big roles and was ready for the demands that such a part entailed. All of her hard work to gain recognition came to a horrific end, however, when she was brutally murdered on October 30th, 1982.

On that Day

It was after her work on "Poltergeist" came to a close that Dominique Dunne began seeing a guy by the name of John Thomas Sweeney. Mr. Sweeney was a successful chef who catered to the stars. Sweeney was apparently an attractive and charismatic guy, but soon after Dominique moved in with the man, he began to show his darker side. He became abusive and controlling.

At one point, after a particularly bad argument, Dominque sought shelter at her Mom's house. But it wasn't long before Sweeney tracked her down. Despite her mother yelling at him to get off of the property, Sweeney began banging on doors and windows, trying to get inside. It was only when Dominque's mother mentioned calling the cops, that Sweeney finally took off.

Unfortunately, the con-man managed to convince Dominique to come back to him. It was a decision that she immediately regretted. Despite his promises that he could change, rather than get better, Sweeney's abuse only got worse. And on September 26th of that year, John Sweeney nearly killed Dominque Dunne. During an argument, he knocked her to the ground, got on top of her, and started to choke her.

Fortunately for Dunne, a friend was actually staying with them at the time and was alert enough to overhear the struggle that was taking place. This friend was also brave enough to confront this madman, and get him to stop what he was doing. Dunne survived this attack and realized that she had to get away from her abuser before it was too late. She finally made up her mind to leave and end the relationship for good.

Sweeney remained obsessed with getting Dominique back, however, and tried repeatedly to get her to change her mind. It was after her refusal to go along with one of his latest attempts to patch things up, on October 30th, 1982, that John Sweeney lost control, leaped upon his ex-girlfriend, and choked her to death in her own driveway, right in front of her home.

Dominque didn't die immediately, however, and was rushed off to the hospital. Here she remained in a vegetative state. After she was declared brain dead, her parents made the painful decision, to pull the plug on her life support a few days later. Her birthday was coming up in just a few weeks and had she lived long enough to see her next birthday, she would have been 23 years old.

The Investigation

There wasn't much of a need for an investigation in this case, since it was clear from the very beginning who the main suspect was. There was little doubt that Dominique's estranged ex-boyfriend John Sweeney, was the killer. Once the police arrived on the scene, in fact, they found Sweeney right there, with hands upraised, openly declaring, "I killed my girlfriend."

The Suspect

John Sweeney was arrested and stood trial for Dunne's death, but in the end, since his actions were an obvious crime of passion, he was not charged with murder. Sweeney who was known to get so enraged that he blacked out, convincingly made the case, that he was so angry arguing with the actress, that he couldn't remember what happened. He insisted that he did indeed blackout, and the next thing he knew he had his hands on Dunne's throat.

In the End

Sweeney confessed to killing Dunne but insisted that it was accidental and that he was in such a blind rage at the time, that he could not even recall much of what happened. The jury believed much of Sweeney's testimony and on September 21st, 1983, the more serious charge of second-degree murder was thrown out. Instead, he was hit up with a charge of "voluntary manslaughter." For this, he was sentenced to just six years in prison.

He would ultimately be let out after serving just three and a half years behind bars. Incredibly enough, Sweeney was then able to just pick up and move on with his life. He eventually even landed a great job as a head chef at a prestigious restaurant. This end result from Sweeney's actions was an outrage to many and remains controversial to this day.

The Allure of Tinseltown

The lights of Hollywood have lured many a star to Tinseltown. For those who don't know, the appellation of "Tinseltown" actually alludes to the perception of Hollywood having a surreal, glittery sheen like "tinsel." But the glare of these alluring lights has also attracted the eyes of those with less than benign intentions at heart. And both celebrities— and those aspiring to become one—have been ensnared by the predators that lurk in the foothills of Hollywood.

Kristi Johnson was a prime example of this. She was a smart, attractive young woman with a lot going for her. Normally she was very careful about who she met and kept random admiring men at a distance. But when a guy who called himself "Victor Thomas" waltzed up to her with a proposal to make her a star—heck, to even get her a part in a James Bond film no less—she couldn't resist the opportunity that was being presented. But the opportunity proved to be a lie, and once she was in this malevolent fraudster's grip, it was too late.

Even those who are already established in Hollywood can find themselves unable to flee from the negative undercurrents of Tinseltown. All the way back in 1922, promising director James Desmond Taylor was accosted by someone who decided to end his life. The killer was never caught, but a string of suspects still haunts this case to this very day.

It's sad whenever *anyone's* life comes to a tragic end, but when it's a famous icon who perishes, that pain can be magnified and felt by millions. It might sound silly, at first glance, for folks to mourn over famous Hollywood celebrities—that they have never met—but for them, the pain is real all the same. Just consider the slain singer Selena, who had thousands of fans not only mourn her death, but some who considered becoming vigilantes themselves, just in case her killer escaped.

The very same thing occurred when martial arts legend Bruce Lee perished, with many fans and admirers calling the foul play and demanding justice for a man whom they had never met, yet deeply felt was a part of their own family. It's equally distressing when celebrities themselves become suspected of murder, as was the case when Robert Blake was suspected of killing his wife, Bonny Bakely. Or when Phil Spector was convicted of killing Lana Clarkson.

No one expects our heroes of film and music to end up on the wrong side of the law. And even the thought of their guilt might make us think twice before watching their films or listening to their records. It's the draw of celebrity that has that kind of power over us. We put our stars up on a pedestal and admire their gleam, only to have to avert our eyes should they tragically fall.

Then there are suspicious Hollywood deaths that have never even been proven to be murdered in the first place. We are told that the guy who played Superman on TV—George Reeves—spontaneously decided to take his own life on the slightest of whims. Yet, there are consistent rumors that his death was actually a mob hit, orchestrated by Hollywood insider Eddie Mannix. Rumors that were

168

allegedly bolstered when his former wife Toni Mannix allegedly admitted to as much, on her own death bed.

Tinseltown can indeed be a scary place. And whether you're a celebrity, aspiring to be one, or simply passing through—you might want to be on your guard. Because Hollywood can be hazardous to your health. Not every smiling face is what it might seem to be in Tinseltown.

Image Credits

Bob Crane photo
By Maury Foldare and Associates-public relations-appears to be for Bing Crosby Productions, the show producer. - eBay itemphoto frontphoto back, Public Domain, https://commons.wikimedia.org/w/index.php?curid=19791929

Phil Hartman photo
By Paul Hartmann - Original image e-mailed to uploader (Gran2) with GFDL license on 2010-05-31, in response to an e-mail request., CC BY-SA 3.0, https://commons.wikimedia.org/w/index.php?curid=10509212

George Reeves photo
By U.S. Treasury Department - United States Treasury Department film, Public Domain, https://commons.wikimedia.org/w/index.php?curid=97701612

William Desmond Taylor photo
By Albert Witzel - icollector.com, Public Domain, https://commons.wikimedia.org/w/index.php?curid=73215161

Bruce Lee photo
By National General Pictures - eBayfrontback, Public Domain, https://commons.wikimedia.org/w/index.php?curid=35945400

Natalie Wood photo
By Allan warren - Own work, CC BY-SA 3.0, https://commons.wikimedia.org/w/index.php?curid=12757150

Marvin Gaye photo
By Photograph by Jim Britt, whose other (copyrighted) photos of Gaye from the same session—many of them in full color—can be seen at his website. Originally distributed by Motown Records. - Scan via NYTimes. Retouched by uploader., Public Domain, https://commons.wikimedia.org/w/index.php?curid=96235514

Rebecca Schaeffer photo
By CBS Network - ebay.com, front of photo, back of photo, Public Domain, https://commons.wikimedia.org/w/index.php?curid=36650018

Sharon Tate photo
By 20th Century-Fox; Restored by Adam Cuerden - eBayfrontback, Public Domain, https://commons.wikimedia.org/w/index.php?curid=90441108

Made in the USA
Las Vegas, NV
15 December 2021